FINLAND
in Pictures

Francesca Davis DiPiazza

Twenty-First Century Books

Contents

Lerner Publishing Group, Inc., realizes that current information and statistics quickly become out of date. To extend the usefulness of the Visual Geography Series, we developed www.vgsbooks.com, a website offering links to up-to-date information, as well as in-depth material, on a wide variety of subjects. All the websites listed on www.vgsbooks.com have been carefully selected by researchers at Lerner Publishing Group, Inc. However, Lerner Publishing Group, Inc., is not responsible for the accuracy or suitability of the material on any website other than www.lernerbooks.com. It is recommended that students using the Internet be supervised by a parent or teacher. Links on www.vgsbooks.com will be regularly reviewed and updated as needed.

Website address: www.lernerbooks.com

Twenty-First Century Books
A division of Lerner Publishing Group, Inc.
241 First Avenue North
Minneapolis, MN 55401 U.S.A.

web enhanced @ www.vgsbooks.com

Library of Congress Cataloging-in-Publication Data

DiPiazza, Francesca, 1961–
    Finland in pictures / by Francesca Davis DiPiazza.
       p. cm. — (Visual geography series)
    Includes bibliographical references and index.
    ISBN 978-0-7613-4626-5 (lib. bdg. : alk. paper)
    1. Finland—Juvenile literature. I. Title.
   DL1012.D46 2011
   948.97–dc22   2009004944

Manufactured in the United States of America
1 – BP – 7/15/10

INTRODUCTION

The Republic of Finland is a country in northern Europe. Its capital city, Helsinki, is the northernmost capital on the continent. Finland's northern region, Lapland, is in the Arctic (near the North Pole). Colorful northern lights there streak the winter sky, and the midnight sun brightens summer nights. The Sami are Lapland's indigenous, or native, people. A small minority in Finland, the Sami's ancestors were mainly reindeer herders.

For many generations, Finland's vast forests provided a livelihood for many Finns. In the twenty-first century, about 70 percent of Finland's 5.3 million people live in cities. But Finns value their land's unspoiled, natural beauty. They work to protect their forests, lakes, and seacoast.

Once a poor farming country, modern Finland is a highly industrialized nation. Nokia and other high-tech businesses are world leaders in cell phone and information technology. Tourism is also an important money earner. Visitors enjoy Finland's natural splendors and many national parks. They hike nature trails in summer

and cross-country ski in winter.

For much of its history, Finland was caught in the middle of a power struggle between its western neighbor, Sweden, and its eastern neighbor, Russia. The Swedish Empire ruled Finland from the mid-1200s until 1808. In that year, the Russian Empire took over Finland. However, Russia allowed the Finns to keep their own laws and religions.

Finns' pride in their culture grew in the 1800s, along with a desire to have their own nation. In the 1830s, a collection of ancient legends called the *Kalevala* added to a growing sense of Finnish national identity. It helped to spark a creative era that Finns call their Golden Age. The composer Jean Sibelius wrote the inspiring music of *Finlandia* in 1899. Golden Age art and design from Finland came to the world's attention at the 1900 Paris World's Fair.

In 1917 Russian revolutionaries overthrew the Russian czar (ruler) as a first step in forming the Soviet Union (a union of republics that included Russia). That year Finland declared its independence from Russia.

Finland
International border
Capital city
City
Point of interest
National park
0
100 Miles
0
100 KM
N
NORWAY
Pechenga (Petsamo)
Inari
Muonio River
Enontekiö
SWEDEN
LAPLAND
RUSSIA
Tornio River
ARCTIC CIRCLE
Rovaniemi
Kemi River
Kemi
Oulu
Oulu River
Lake Oulu
KARELIA
Sonkajärvi
Gulf of Bothnia
Vaasa
Seinäjoki
Jyväskylä
Lake Näsi
Savonlinna
SWEDEN
Pori
Tampere
Lake Saimaa
Lahti
Hämeenlinna
Saimaa Canal
Riihimäki
Vyborg
ÅLAND ISLANDS
Somero
Nuuksio National Park
Jokela
Turku
Kotka
Espoo
Helsinki
Kauniainen
Suomenlinna
Saint Petersburg
TURKU ARCHIPELAGO
Gulf of Finland
RUSSIA
Baltic Sea
ESTONIA
0
500 Miles
0
500 KM
ICELAND
ATLANTIC OCEAN
Scandinavian Peninsula
FINLAND
RUSSIA
DENMARK
POLAND
GERMANY
EUROPE
AFRICA

The small, new nation of Finland tried to avoid conflicts with its powerful eastern neighbor. But early in World War II (1939–1945), the Soviet Union attacked Finland. Finns fought to defend their freedom. After the Finnish defeat in 1944, the nation lost some territory but kept its independence.

Experts say that—give or take a few million—Finnish forests contain 77 billion trees, each at least 4 feet (1.3 meters) tall.

The victorious Soviets demanded large payments in money and goods from Finland. To meet the demand, the Finns modernized their industries. People moved to the cities in large numbers for work. By the early 1950s, Finland was no longer a poor farming country. It even paid off its war debts to the Soviet Union early. In 1952 Helsinki showed off its successes when it hosted the Olympic Games.

Since that time, Finland has made peace a top priority. In 1995 Finland joined the European Union—a group of countries in Europe that work together for peace and prosperity.

Finns also value social equality. They elected their first female president, Tarja Halonen, in 2000 and reelected her in 2006. Her career has focused on issues of social justice. The former president, Martti Ahtisaari, won the Nobel Peace Prize in 2008. He had worked for many years to settle conflicts around the world. That same year, a political scandal arose over Finnish politicians' election funding. Even so, Finland remains one of the least corrupt societies in the world.

Finns work hard and enjoy a good standard of living. They pay high taxes to guarantee health care and other social services for all. This results in some of the best health statistics in the world. Finland stresses the importance of education. Finns excel in research and development of computer software and other modern technology. The nation's strong economy is a tribute to a well-educated workforce. Finns are proud of their traditions and their independence. They look forward to continuing success as members of the European Union.

 Visit www.vgsbooks.com for links to websites with up-to-the-minute information about Finland as well as downloadable maps and photographs of Finland.

THE LAND

Finland is part of the large Scandinavian Peninsula. A peninsula is an arm of land surrounded on three sides by water. The country is called Suomi in Finnish. It covers 130,128 square miles (337,030 square kilometers) of territory—including its mainland, islands, and inland waters. Finland is about half the size of Texas. It extends about 700 miles (1,120 km) from north to south and about 400 miles (640 km) east to west. One-third of the country lies in the Arctic, the region around the North Pole.

Finland is one of five nations in northern Europe called the Nordic countries. Finland's neighbors Norway, to the far north, and Sweden, to the west, are also Nordic countries. (Denmark and Iceland are the other two Nordic countries.) Besides their location, the Nordic countries share similar social systems. Russia runs along Finland's entire eastern border, for 793 miles (1,276 km). Russia has a different social and political history than the Nordic countries and western Europe.

The Baltic Sea wraps around 777 miles (1,250 km) of Finland's southern shores. The Gulf of Bothnia—an arm of the Baltic Sea—separates Finland from Sweden to the west. The Gulf of Finland, another arm of the Baltic, washes against Finland's southeastern coast. The country of Estonia lies only about 50 miles (80 km) across this gulf, to the south.

Finland also includes Europe's largest archipelago, or group of islands. About eighty thousand islands lie off the southwestern coast. The large Åland Islands group sits between Finland and Sweden. The islands form an autonomous (self-governing) Finnish region. Swedish is the main language on the Ålands.

◎ Topography

Thousands of years ago, glaciers—slow-moving ice masses—completely covered Finland. The miles-high ice carved out valleys and smoothed down peaks. Its movement also dug shallow beds for thousands of lakes.

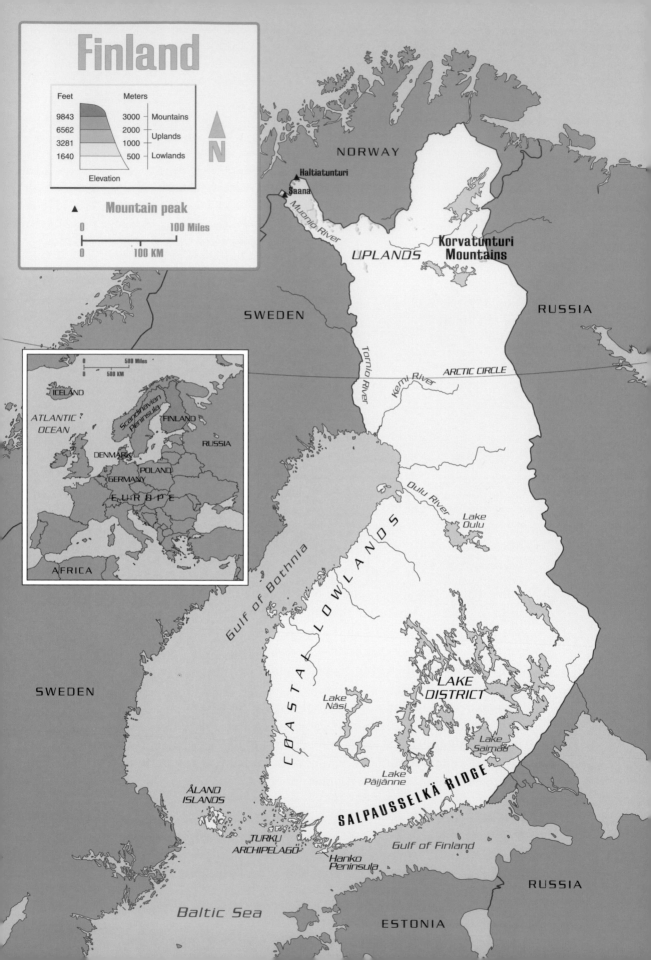

Finland

Feet | Meters
9843 | 3000 | Mountains
6562 | 2000 | Uplands
3281 | 1000 | Lowlands
1640 | 500

Elevation

▲ Mountain peak

0   100 Miles
0   100 KM

N

NORWAY

▲ Haltiatunturi
◢ Saana

Muonio River

UPLANDS

Korvatunturi
Mountains

SWEDEN

RUSSIA

Tornio River

Kemi River

ARCTIC CIRCLE

ICELAND

ATLANTIC
OCEAN

Scandinavian
Peninsula

FINLAND

RUSSIA

DENMARK

POLAND

GERMANY

E U R O P E

AFRICA

0   500 Miles
0   500 KM

Oulu River

Lake
Oulu

Gulf of Bothnia

C O A S T A L   L O W L A N D S

SWEDEN

Lake
Näsi

LAKE
DISTRICT

Lake
Saimaa

Lake
Päijänne

ÅLAND
ISLANDS

SALPAUSSELKÄ RIDGE

TURKU
ARCHIPELAGO

Hanko
Peninsula

Gulf of Finland

RUSSIA

Baltic Sea

ESTONIA

The ice receded about ten thousand years ago. It left a fairly flat land, much of it swampy and dotted with lakes. Only 8 percent of Finnish land is suitable for crop farming.

Finland has three main topographic, or landscape, regions. They are the Uplands region in the north, the central Lake District, and the Coastal Lowlands in the south and west.

The Uplands average about 1,500 feet (457 m) above sea level. They rise north of the Artic Circle in the region of Lapland. The highest hills are formed of hard granite rock. Swamps and marshes separate many of the northern hills from one another. Finland's highest peak—Haltiatunturi—reaches 4,344 feet (1,324 m) near the Norwegian border. The region also contains some of the country's vast forests. Home to the Sami people, the region is sparsely populated.

Finland's Lake District begins south of the Arctic Circle (the border of the Arctic region). Most of the terrain is lowland that slopes gradually southward to the coasts. Forests of birch, spruce, and pine cover large sections of the Lake District. The lakes contain thousands of islands. Many of them are very small. Some Finns own their own island and build summer homes there.

When the glaciers melted away, they left behind long, level ridges of sand and rock—called eskers—throughout Finland. The largest eskers make up the Salpausselkä Ridge. It stretches from the Hanko Peninsula in southern Finland to the Russian border. In some places, the ridge is 600 feet (183 m) high. Roads run along the narrow ridge. Salpausselkä provides gravel and rock for building materials. Lower

The Saana fjeld, or mountain, is in the region of Lapland in northern Finland. Reindeer are native to this part of Finland.

eskers serve as level roadbeds across many of Finland's lakes and swamps.

The Coastal Lowlands form a 20- to 60-mile-wide (32 to 96 km) band along the seashore. In western Finland, the coastal region is flat. In the southeast, low hills and valleys vary the terrain along the Gulf of Finland. Finland's capital, Helsinki, is in this region. The fertile soil in the coastal plain supports the country's most productive farms. Most of Finland's population live in this region.

The last glaciers melted about ten thousand years ago. Freed from the heavy load of ice, Finland's ground slowly began to rise from sea level. In places along the western coast, this postglacial rebound continues. The rebound lifts more land from the sea at the rate of about 1 foot (0.3 m) every fifty years. Some ports in areas that have risen up, such as Pori in the southwest, have had to extend their harbors farther to reach the sea.

Lakes and Rivers

Lakes and rivers take up 10 percent of Finland's total land surface. Marshes occupy about 17 percent. Altogether, inland waters occupy 12,206 square miles (31,614 sq. km) of Finland. The main lakes link up to form connected waterways. Rivers run in and out of the lakes. Boats travel on these waterways. Cars cross them on ferryboats or bridges. Drivers must travel long distances on roads around the largest lakes, however.

Finland's largest lake, Saimaa, is in the southeast. Ships transport timber and goods on Lake Saimaa and its network of rivers. The Saimaa Canal connects this lake-and-river system to the Russian port of Vyborg on the Gulf of Finland.

Finland's other important water networks include the Lake Päijänne system in south central Finland and the Lake Näsi network in the southwest. Travelers in the west central section of the country use the lakes and rivers of the Oulu system.

One of Finland's nicknames is **Land of 50,000 Lakes**. To be correct, it should be **Land of 187,888 Lakes**. Most of the lakes are small, but 309 of them are larger than 4 square miles (10 sq. km).

Finland has numerous rivers. Many dams harness the power of rushing water to produce hydroelectricity. The major rivers are in the uplands of the north and west. The longest waterway is the Kemi River. It flows for 330 miles (531 km) through southern Lapland and enters the Gulf of Bothnia at the town of Kemi. Another waterway that supplies hydroelectric power is the Oulu River. It joins the sea 60 miles (96 km) south of Kemi. The Tornio River and its tributary (branch), the Muonio, together

Lake Saimaa, the largest lake in Finland, covers more than 1,660 square miles (4,300 sq. km) of land in southeastern Finland. Most of the lake looks like this, with twisting waterways and thousands of islands.

make up the second-longest river system in Finland. They form the country's boundary with Sweden.

Most rivers in Finland are short and not well suited to boat travel. In addition, thousands of rapids prevent boats from crossing many of the nation's waterways. To overcome this, Finns have built canals to bypass the rough parts of the rivers.

▶ Climate

Finland has four seasons, with a great variety of weather. Winter is the longest season. In Lapland, snow may fall as early as September and not disappear until May. February is the coldest month in the country. It brings average temperatures of 5°F (–15°C) in the north. Sometimes it gets as cold as –40°F (–40°C). The western seacoast has warmer winters than expected for its northern location. A warm ocean current called the North Atlantic Current heats the western winter winds. This keeps coastal temperatures around 25°F (–4°C). Southern inland temperatures average 13°F (–10°C). Wintry eastern winds from Russia can bring severe cold to eastern and central Finland. Lake water freezes so thick that cars can drive on the ice. Occasionally, an arctic winter freezes the entire Gulf of Bothnia. Special ships called icebreakers keep shipping lanes on the gulfs and the inland waterways open.

THE ARCTIC CIRCLE

The Arctic Circle is a line on Earth's map that marks the Arctic region. Above this line, the sun doesn't set at midsummer. This "polar day" is known as the Midnight Sun. And at midwinter, the sun doesn't rise. Due to changes in Earth's tilt, the edges of the circle shift, but the Finnish region of Lapland is mostly within the Arctic. Like crossing the equator at Earth's center, travelers consider crossing the Arctic Circle to be a special, even magical, event. Visitors to Lapland may go through a ceremony and get a certificate when they enter the circle.

In the far north, the sun does not rise for fifty-one days during the winter, though light does come over the horizon. Arcs of the aurora borealis, or northern lights, often play across the winter nighttime sky. Finns call the lights fox fire. The name comes from a Sami legend about a fox that sends sparks into the sky when its tail strikes snowdrifts.

Spring brings dramatic changes. It often comes quickly, rapidly thawing ice and snow. Summers are short. Breezes from the Baltic Sea cool Finland's southern coasts. Inland, Finland's many lakes and forests offset the warm air currents from Russia. July is the warmest month. The average temperature is 63°F (17°C) in the south and 60°F (15°C) in the north. Lake water temperatures can reach 68°F (20°C), comfortable for swimming.

The beautiful, brightly colored **aurora borealis** (northern lights) can often be seen flickering across the night sky in the Lapland region during wintertime.

Because Finland lies so far north, its summer days are long. In the extreme north, the sun does not set for seventy-three days. In fact, Lapland is called the Land of the Midnight Sun. Even in southern Finland, the sun stays above the horizon for nineteen hours at midsummer.

Autumn brings beautiful colors to Finland's forests. Hiking in Lapland is popular in this season.

Southern Finland receives about 28 inches (71 centimeters) of rainfall annually. About 18 inches (46 cm) fall in the north. August is usually the rainiest month. About one-third of the annual precipitation falls as snow.

Flora and Fauna

Forests cover about 70 percent of Finland. Evergreen trees—mostly spruce and pine—grow through most of the country. Throughout most of Finland, bushes yield lingonberries, crowberries, and cloudberries in the summer. Mushrooms flourish on forest floors. Maples, elms, ashes, lindens, and hazels thrive in southern Finland. Stands of Norway pines dominate the area just north of the Arctic Circle. They give way to dwarf birches and alders in the far north, at the timberline (the outer limit of places where weather conditions support trees). Above the timberline, hardy shrubs, mosses, and lichens blanket the hillsides.

Finland's most abundant furry animals are red squirrels, muskrats, pine martens, and foxes. Wolves and brown bears survive mostly in eastern and northern Finland. Moose and elk also inhabit the country. These large animals pose a serious hazard to drivers. An average of ten Finns die every year in car crashes with moose.

Reindeer once roamed wild in Lapland. They provided the region's residents—the Sami—with milk, meat, and clothing. Domesticated reindeer have replaced the wild herds. Lapland is also home to the lemming, a small rodent about 5 inches (13 cm) long. Lemmings stay active all winter. Their long soft fur and furry feet keep

Lingonberries grow throughout most of Finland. They are very tart and are most often made into jam.

them warm. There is a popular—but inaccurate—belief that lemmings commit mass suicide by leaping off cliffs. When lemming populations rise too high, they migrate in large numbers. Though they can swim, some of them drown crossing rivers and lakes.

The Saimaa ringed seal lives only in Lake Saimaa. Overhunting and pollution endanger this species, and fewer than three hundred survive.

The country's waters contain many fish, including pike and perch. Salmon live in large lakes or offshore, returning to rivers to breed. Codfish, eel, flounder, and sea trout are among the fish that live in the Baltic Sea. This inland sea is not as salty as an open ocean. Some sea life evolved differently in the less salty water. The Baltic herring, for instance, is smaller than Atlantic herring.

The nation's many lakes are also breeding grounds for mosquitoes. Finland's mosquitoes don't carry diseases, but they are an annoyance all summer.

Bird-watchers in Finland keep an eye out for the country's 450 kinds of birds. Finland is on the path of birds migrating to and from the Arctic. The sight of migrating swans inspired a piece of music by Jean Sibelius, Finland's most famous composer. Waterbirds include storm petrels, divers, and cormorants. Eagles, vultures, hawks, and owls are raptors, or birds that hunt and eat other animals. Game birds—grouse, wild ducks, and ptarmigan—are plentiful.

A brown bear and her cubs walk through a bog in northern Finland. The brown bear is Finland's national animal. *Inset:* The Saimaa ringed seal, found only in the freshwater of Lake Saimaa, has been protected under Finnish law since 1955.

Visit www.vgsbooks.com for links to websites with additional information about the northern lights, as well as links to websites about Finland's weather, plants and animals, and more.

Natural Resources and Environmental Issues

Forests are Finland's most important natural resource. Foresters harvest trees for timber, paper, and pulp. The country's minerals include iron ore, copper, nickel, lead, zinc, cobalt, and tin. Gold is the leading export metal.

Finns want to conserve their natural environment. With a healthy economy, Finland can afford to preserve 8 percent of its land, including 13 percent of its forests. This is the highest rate in Europe. Thirty-five national parks protect the nation's unspoiled wilderness areas.

As an industrialized country, Finland creates its share of pollution. Farming wastes and toxins from Finnish factories pollute the water. Russian industries also pollute gulf waters around Finland. Coal-burning industries send pollutants into the air that create acid rain. This toxic precipitation kills vast stands of pines, endangering Finland's forests.

Finnish wildlife is still abundant, but hunters and farmers have greatly reduced animal populations. The government has passed laws to protect some animals, such as Saimaa ringed seals. Boats, fishing nets, and pollution from factories and summer cottages endanger the seals. Global climate changes are further threats. The seals raise their young in snow nests, which insulate them from cold. As temperatures rise, there is less snow, and fewer pups survive the winter.

Finland's many river dams interfere with salmon migration. These fish return to the rivers where they were born to spawn their eggs. Finns have built salmon gates, somewhat like locks for boats. The stepped gates allow the fish to travel upriver. Pollution and overfishing in the Baltic reduces the number of wild salmon and other fish.

Cities

More than 63 percent of Finland's 5.3 million people live in urban areas, mostly in the south. Many midsized towns exist along the coasts. Northern Finland is sparsely populated. No city in Finland rivals the capital of Helsinki in size and importance.

HELSINKI (population 577,000) sits on a rugged granite peninsula on the Gulf of Finland. It is the northernmost capital on the continent

The city of **Helsinki**, pictured here with a view from the Helsinki Harbor, was founded in 1550. It became Finland's capital in 1812.

of Europe. (The capital of the island nation of Iceland is farther north.) Many offshore islands are near the city. The cultural center of Finland, Helsinki contains museums, art galleries, and educational institutions. Most large Finnish businesses have their headquarters in Helsinki. The city's chief industries are shipbuilding, engineering, porcelain making, and textile manufacturing.

Helsinki has a long and complicated history. Both Sweden and Russia controlled the site at different times. Fire destroyed most of the city in 1808. In 1816 the government hired a German architect, C. L. Engel, to rebuild it. Engel created a spacious city with broad streets; large parks; and tall, white buildings. Later designers also planned many of the capital's residential areas. An underground railway links the suburbs to central Helsinki. It helps to limit urban traffic.

ESPOO (population 242,000) is Finland's second-largest city. It is immediately to Helsinki's west, on the coast of the Gulf of Finland. The city's oldest-standing building is the Espoo Cathedral, a church dating from 1480. The city grew rapidly after World War II and became an industrial center. Espoo is home to the Helsinki University of Technology and the world headquarters of Nokia, the cell phone company.

TAMPERE (population 210,000) is in south central Finland. A long series of rapids called the Tammerkoski divides the town. Dams on the waterway provide the city with electricity. Founded by Sweden in

1779, Tampere grew into an important industrial town in the 1800s. In modern times, it manufactures footwear, leather goods, textiles, metal products, and paper. Modern Tampere also has a university and a college of technology. Many rock and heavy metal bands have come from Tampere.

TURKU (population 176,000) is an important port and manufacturing hub in the southwest. It is Finland's oldest city and was the country's capital until the early 1800s. Turku sits on the Gulf of Bothnia, very close to Sweden. Swedish is the main language of about 5 percent of the inhabitants.

ROVANIEMI (population 59,000) is the capital of Lapland. German troops burned most of the city in 1945. The rebuilt city includes buildings designed by Finnish architect Alvar Aalto. Close to the Arctic Circle, the city attracts many tourists.

BACK TO THE SEA

A friendly rivalry exists between the inland city of Tampere and Turku, on the coast. Turku experiences post-glacial rebound, which means the city's land continues to rise from the sea. Once a year, a small group of students from Tampere jump on Turku's city square in a joking effort to push the city back into the sea.

Rovaniemi, because of its location near the Arctic Circle, is a popular Christmas destination.

HISTORY AND GOVERNMENT

People first came to Finland toward the end of the last ice age, about ten thousand years ago. At that time, glaciers were still shaping parts of the country and a freshwater lake occupied the Baltic Sea. Some historians believe the earliest inhabitants are the ancestors of the Sami. They lived along the coasts of southern Finland, fishing and hunting wild animals for food. Relics from their time indicate that they built boats and decorated the prows with carvings of moose heads.

▷ New Immigrants Arrive

About 3500 B.C., new groups of people began crossing from northern and central Russia to the Baltic Sea region. They were nomads, or people who move seasonally from place to place seeking food and water for their animal herds. Known as the Finno-Ugric peoples, their language is the ancestor of modern Finnish. They gradually spread northward in Finland. They pushed the country's original inhabitants even farther north.

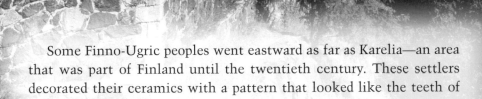

Some Finno-Ugric peoples went eastward as far as Karelia—an area that was part of Finland until the twentieth century. These settlers decorated their ceramics with a pattern that looked like the teeth of a comb.

By 1200 B.C., contact with outsiders had brought knowledge of bronze to Finland. By 200 B.C., Finnish peoples were making iron tools and weapons. In this era, Germanic groups reached Finland from northern Europe. Historians call these newcomers the boat-axe peoples, after the shape of their polished stone axes. As the boat-axe peoples spread over large parts of southwestern Finland, they inter-married with the original population.

According to ancient folktales, some Iron Age people in southwestern Finland called themselves Suomalaiset. They named their homeland Suomi, the name Finns still use. They hunted wild animals for survival. Another group, the Hämäläiset, lived inland in an area that extended from present-day Lahti to Tampere. They were farmers. The third main group of Finns—the Karelians—dwelt along the eastern border of modern Finland. Large areas of wilderness separated each group.

Scandinavian influences came to Finland in A.D. 800. Fleets of Swedish adventurers called Vikings came to mainland Finland. Some moved on into Karelia. By 862 the Vikings had established trading outposts at Novgorod (in modern-day Russia).

Through these trade links, the Karelians made contact with the Byzantine Empire, far to the south in modern-day Turkey. The Byzantine culture and religion influenced Karelian society. It developed somewhat differently than western Finland.

⊙ Swedish Rule

By the 1100s, Sweden had become a unified kingdom. Swedish traders brought their culture to the Suomalaiset and the Hämäläiset in Finland's west. In 1155 King Erik of Sweden tried to force the Roman Catholic faith on Finland, whose people worshipped many nature gods. The king also wanted to end Finland's raids along Sweden's coast.

Finland's three main groups were not united and could not defend themselves against Sweden. To achieve his two aims, Erik conquered southwest Finland. He left Henry—a bishop, or a church official, from Sweden—in charge of religious affairs at Turku.

During the thirteenth century, under the Swedish noble Birger Jarl, Sweden extended its control farther eastward. Jarl built the castle of Hämeenlinna at a strategic point on the Salpausselkä Ridge. This was Finland's main east-west trade route.

As the Swedes expanded into eastern Finland, they met opposition from the Russians. The Russians had gained rule of Novgorod and also claimed Karelia. In 1323 Sweden and Russia signed the Treaty of Pähkinäsaari, which divided the territory. Sweden gave up the eastern part of Karelia to the Russians. But battles continued between the two powers until 1351. In that year, they signed another treaty that gave Sweden unchallenged control of Finland.

After peace took hold, many Swedish settlers moved to the west and the south of Finland. The Swedes set up their own legal and governmental systems. The Swedish language came into common use, especially among farmers, local officials, and the wealthy. Turku became the capital of the Swedish province of Finland.

By the 1400s, the bishops at Turku had persuaded most Finns to become Roman Catholic. The Finnish belief in many gods gradually yielded to the one-god Christian faith. The Karelians, however, joined the Orthodox branch of the Christian religion, from the Byzantine Empire.

◉ Gains and Losses

As Swedish subjects, the Finnish peoples became more unified throughout the 1400s and 1500s. Many saw themselves as part of Sweden, like the Swedes. During these centuries, a powerful Swedish-speaking but Finnish-born ruling class arose in Finland. A few Finnish nobles helped organize Sweden's finances and rebuild its navy. Other Finns became judges in local courts. Finnish officials governed castles in Finland for Swedish kings. Many Finns lived and worked in Sweden's capital city of Stockholm. Finns sent representatives to the Swedish legislature and were active in the royal government at the highest levels.

Lacking its own university, Finland sent its best students to study in other parts of Europe in the 1500s. The Finnish scholar and bishop Mikael Agricola, for example, studied at the German university in Wittenberg. Agricola translated the Bible's New Testament into Finnish.

He also introduced Finns to the religious ideas of Martin Luther and the Protestant Reformation. This movement challenged the authority of the Roman Catholic Church. In many parts of northern Europe, including Finland, the Lutheran sect of Protestantism became popular in the sixteenth century.

This statue in Turku, Finland, commemorates the bishop and reformer **Mikael Agricola,** who is considered the father of written Finnish.

During the early 1600s, the Swedish king Gustavus Adolphus used his army to make Sweden a great power in the Baltic region. The king's military expeditions relied on the fighting skills of Finnish soldiers. Sweden tightened its control over Finland and heavily taxed the Finns to pay for the army.

In this century, battles, hunger, and taxation made life hard for Finns. Most people struggled to survive as poor farmers. Clearing trees for farmland was backbreaking work. The diet was poor too. Ground fish bones and birch-tree bark were often the only ingredients available for bread making. Much-needed seasonal work came from hunting seals or harvesting pine tar. Tar was the main product Finland sold to other nations. The sticky stuff protects and seals wood. It was also an ingredient in soaps and skin medicine. Workers cut pine trees and boiled down the tar in special pits. They sent barrels of tar on boats downriver to seaports.

Gustavus Adolphus died in 1632. The new government sent Per Brahe to serve as the governor-general of Finland at Turku. Brahe gave his energies and loyalty to the Finns. He encouraged the use of the Finnish language, rather than Swedish. In 1640 he established Finland's first university, at Turku.

By 1658, when Brahe retired, Sweden was fighting to extend its territory and to limit Russian expansion. While the Swedish army fought elsewhere, Russia invaded Finland. The Finns, fighting to protect their homeland, defeated the Russians. In 1660 Sweden and Russia signed the Treaty of Kardis. It set the eastern boundary of Finland.

In 1672 the young Swedish king Karl XI expanded the use of the Swedish language in Finland and strengthened the province's ties to Swedish culture. The Swedish monarch also gave the bishop of Turku responsibility

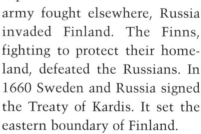

Swedish soldier and statesman Per Brahe the Younger made many positive changes in Finland while he served as governor-general. In 1638 he introduced a postal system and founded ten new towns in the 1640s and 1650s.

for teaching all Finns to read and write. The bishop and his priests took this duty seriously. As a result of their work, Finland became one of the first countries in Europe to achieve almost complete literacy.

Except for the spread of education, Finland made little progress in the late 1600s. Swedish rulers increasingly neglected their Finnish subjects, who were providing soldiers and paying taxes to Sweden. In addition to these burdens, famine struck Finland in 1696 and 1697. Hunger and disease killed one-third of the population in those two years.

▶ Wrath and War

In 1670 the Swedish army attacked Poland. Russia sided with Poland against Sweden. The long conflict is known as the Great Northern War (1700–1721). Sweden's motive was to cripple Russia, its rival for power in northern Europe.

The war did not go well for Sweden, however. In 1703 the Russian czar, Peter the Great, captured a Swedish fort on the Gulf of Finland. On this site, he began to build the city of Saint Petersburg (called Leningrad, under the Soviet Union). From Saint Petersburg, Russia invaded Finland. Finns called this period of conquest the Great Wrath (1713–1721). By 1718 Russia occupied the entire country. Russian soldiers treated the Finns harshly, destroying settlements and abusing the people. The Russians sent some Finns back to Russia as slaves.

The Peace of Uusikaupunki settled the Great Northern War in 1721. The treaty ended Sweden's role as a major power in northern

This nineteenth-century wood carving depicts the Battle of Poltava in 1709. Russia's decisive victory over Sweden marked the beginning of Russian domination of northern Europe.

Europe. Russia withdrew its forces from Finland but made southeastern Finland, including Karelia, part of Russia.

In a short time, however, fighting broke out again. Russia defeated Sweden and reoccupied Finland. This occupation—known as the Little Wrath—ended with the Peace of Turku in 1743. After this defeat, Sweden lost even more territory in eastern Finland to Russia. The rest of Finland, however, remained under Swedish control.

Years of warfare had damaged Finland's government as well as its economy. Finnish loyalty to Sweden declined. Some people wanted Finland to be independent from Sweden, but there was little support for the idea at the time.

The wars against Russia had shown Sweden that Finland was poorly defended. As a result, Sweden built several fortresses along the seacoast near Helsinki. In 1788 Sweden launched a war against Russia. The war ended in a stalemate in 1790.

The Grand Duchy of Finland

In 1807 the French emperor and general Napoleon was enlarging his empire in Europe. Russia joined France in a war against Great Britain. The two countries tried to force Sweden to close its ports to British ships. Sweden refused, and the Russian czar attacked Finland to punish Sweden. During the resulting Finnish War (1808–1809), the Russians occupied Finland again.

In the peace settlement of 1809, Russia gained full control of all of Finland. Almost seven hundred years of Swedish rule came to an end. The Russian czar, Alexander I, believed that a strong Finland would be a good barrier against Sweden. He called the new territory the Grand Duchy of Finland. A duchy is a land ruled by a duke. In return for keeping their own laws and religions, the Finns accepted the czar as the grand duke of Finland.

Russia returned Karelia and other eastern areas to Finland. In 1812 Alexander moved the duchy's seat of government from Turku, which faced Sweden, to Helsinki. The new capital was only about 100 miles (161 km) from Saint Petersburg, Russia.

Russia mostly let the Grand Duchy of Finland rule itself. Finns elected representatives to a diet (senate) that made laws. Only an elite group of landowning men could vote. Most Finns still worked as farmers who didn't own their land.

The Rise of Nationalism

In the nineteenth century, free from Swedish influence, the Finns began to develop a sense of their own identity. Ideas of creating a Finnish nation went hand in hand with a growing pride in Finnish culture. In the 1830s,

Elias Lönnrot collected and published ancient Finnish folktales from Karelia in a book called the *Kalevala*. This influential work showed Finns their own rich culture. The poet Johan Ludvig Runeberg described the Finnish War in the long patriotic poem *The Tales of Ensign Stål*.

In 1854 Great Britain and France went to war against the Russian Empire. These Western powers fought the Crimean War (1854–1856) to keep Russia from expanding into Turkey. Some Finns favored neutrality—not taking sides—in international affairs. But Finland stayed loyal to Russia and found itself involved in the war. The British navy bombed the Finnish coast. French and British forces invaded the Åland Islands.

The Russian czar Alexander II rewarded Finland's loyalty by giving the country even greater political independence. Finland created its own system of money and formed its own army. Despite nationalistic feelings, Finnish officials were careful not to challenge or anger Russia in any way.

To reflect their national pride, some of the country's leading citizens began to use Finnish as their main language. Johan Vilhelm Snellman set up the first Finnish language schools in the 1860s. Most of the upper and educated classes, however, continued to use Swedish, as did many rural Finns. In 1863 the efforts of Snellman and others forced the government to use Finnish as well as Swedish to carry out official duties.

Elias Lönnrot

THE BIRTH OF FINLAND

In 1848 a wave of nationalism, or patriotic movements for self-rule, swept across Europe. Some historians say that modern Finland was born that year at a students' celebration on May 13. The students had made a flag for the springtime celebration: a lion on a white background. Some consider this Finland's first national flag. A student leader led the gathering in a toast, "To Finland." At the end of the celebration, the students sang "Vårt land" (Our Country). The song would later become Finland's official national anthem. Its lyrics came from the poet Runeberg's *Tales of Ensign Stål*. This was the first clear, public expression of Finnish national identity.

THE GREAT HUNGER YEARS

The last major famine struck Finland in 1866 to 1868. An extra-rainy summer and a long, bitterly cold winter led to widespread crop failures. Starvation and disease killed more than 15 percent of the Finnish population. To stay alive, people made bread from the inner bark of pine trees, mixed with rye flour. Thousands emigrated from Finland, many to the United States. Finns call the famine the Great Hunger Years. Afterward, improvements in farming, transportation, and government prevented similar famines in Finland.

Russia's pro-Finnish attitude changed in 1894, when Czar Nicholas II came to the throne. In 1899 Nicholas ruled that he could impose laws on Finland without the consent of the Finnish Diet. In defense of self-rule, the Finns wrote a document called the Great Address to the czar. Nicholas II overlooked it, and in 1900, he made Russian the official language in Finland. He disbanded Finland's army, and the Russian army began to draft Finns to be soldiers. Finns resisted where they could.

While Finland lost political rights, it gained ground culturally. Finnish art and design won fame at the Paris World's Fair in 1900. Finnish composer Jean Sibelius also won international fame for his rousing new composition *Finlandia*. Nationalists adopted it as their anthem.

Russia tightened its control and limited Finland's independence. In 1905 the Finns used a nationwide work stoppage, called the Great Strike, to oppose Russian control. Russia granted the Finnish demands for an independent parliament (legislature). In 1906 a one-house parliament, called the Eduskunta, replaced the Finnish Diet. For the first time, all adult men and women could vote to elect representatives.

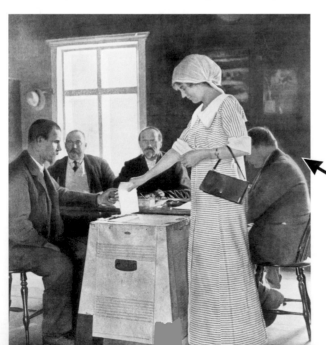

In 1906 Finnish women became the first women in Europe to gain the right to vote—and to run for election. Finns elected nineteen women representatives in their first elections as free citizens, in 1907.

Shortly before World War I (1914–1918) broke out, Russia put Finland under military rule. In the war, Russia sided with Britain and France against Germany.

In March 1917, a revolution in Russia overthrew the czar. In November 1917, Russian revolutionaries called Bolsheviks seized control of Russia's nine-month-old government. Members of the Eduskunta, led by P. E. Svinhufvud, took advantage of Russia's turmoil. They declared independence for Finland on December 6, 1917. Russia accepted Finnish independence within weeks.

Civil War and a New Finland

Finland's birth was stormy. Finns were divided over what type of government to set up. The Reds represented the landless farmers and factory workers. Until 1907 these groups had never held political power. They wanted a Socialist political system like the new Russian government. In theory, such a government would share the wealth and power among all people. The Whites were the Finnish nobility, the army, business owners, and landowners. They wanted to hold on to their power. In January 1918, the split led to the outbreak of the Finnish Civil War. Germany sent aid to the Whites. The Russian Bolsheviks supplied the Reds. Under the Finnish general Carl Gustaf Mannerheim, the Whites defeated the Reds in May 1918. The victory ensured that Finland would remain connected with western Europe, not Russia. About thirty thousand Finns died in the war, mostly on the Reds' side. The war deepened class divisions among Finns that would last for years. World War I ended with the collapse of Germany.

German troops and Finnish supporters take aim at Finnish Red (socialist) snipers in Helsinki during World War I.

Between the Wars

Mannerheim became the temporary head of Finland's government. A new legislature wrote a constitution. On June 17, 1919, the Republic of Finland was born. Citizens elected K. J. Ståhlberg the new nation's first president.

In 1920 the World War I peace conference gave Finland all the territory it had held as a grand duchy in the 1800s. In addition, the nation got a narrow strip of land that led to Petsamo, a port on an arm of the Arctic Ocean. In December 1920, Finland joined the League of Nations. The main goal of this international group was to prevent future wars.

After independence, Finland quickly passed laws providing for freedom of religion, education for all children, and other social programs. Land reforms gave peasants ownership of the plots they farmed. Exports of Finland's forestry products rose, and manufacturing improved.

Finland strengthened its economic ties to the Scandinavian countries—Norway, Sweden, and Denmark—during the 1920s. Meanwhile, Russia and other regions formed the Union of Soviet Socialist Republics, called the USSR, or the Soviet Union.

Finnish culture continued to develop in the 1920s. The Finnish Broadcasting Company and a film industry started up. Finns took up the Argentine tango. They added their own melancholy strains to the music. Finnish runner Paavo Nurmi set world records and won twelve medals at the Olympic Games between 1920 and 1928. The language issue, however, was difficult to settle. Most members of the upper class and many people in rural areas continued to use Swedish, while other Finns demanded the use of Finnish only.

In the 1930s, a worldwide depression hurt Finland's economy. Meanwhile, Germany was growing in power under Nazi leader Adolf Hitler. Germany had helped the anti-Russian White forces during the Finnish Civil War. The Soviet Union feared that the Finns might let Germany go through Finland to attack the USSR. Finland, for its part, was mistrustful of the Soviet Union and began to improve its defenses. To avoid conflict between them, the Soviet Union and Finland signed a nonaggression pact in 1932. It stated that neither country would attack the other. Finland declared that it would stay neutral in foreign affairs.

Three Wars

Despite its desire to stay out of any armed conflicts, Finland ended up fighting three wars during World War II. In August 1939, the Soviet Union and Germany signed the Nazi-Soviet Pact. In the secret agreement, Germany agreed to put Finland in the Soviet sphere of influence.

When Germany invaded Poland in September 1939, World War II broke out. Britain, France, and other nations (later to include the United States) allied against Germany. The Soviet Union at this point stayed out of the war. Finland's suspicions proved right, however. In October 1939, the Soviet leader Joseph Stalin wanted to establish military bases on Finnish territory. Finland refused, and the Soviet Union attacked Finland on November 30. This led to the short but brutal Winter War (1939–1940).

Once again, General Mannerheim led the Finnish army. All Finns pulled together to fight for their country. That winter the temperature fell to a record low of -45°F (–43°C). Many soldiers froze to death. At first the Finnish soldiers inflicted great losses on Soviet troops. Then the Soviets increased their forces and smashed the Finnish army in Karelia. When the Winter War ended in March 1940, Finland lost Karelia.

THE INNER FINN

In the Winter War (1939–1940), the Finns took on the Soviet Union, a nation sixty-six times Finland's size. The Finnish army was hopelessly overpowered by the Soviets. For instance, at the beginning of the war, Finland had 32 tanks to the Soviets' 2,514. Despite this, though they lost some territory, the Finnish army held off a full Soviet invasion. The Finns' success was due to the soldiers' unity and high morale. The Finnish troops were also able to move quickly, with some units traveling on skis. Finns also credit a quality called *sisu*. It comes from a Finnish word that means "inside," but *sisu* means something more like "gutsy." It includes an ability to hold on when the going gets tough. It's a quality that comes in handy living in a cold climate near powerful, sometimes unfriendly neighbors.

Finnish soldiers in the Second World War used skis to move quickly over snow-covered terrain.

General Carl Gustaf Mannerheim *(center)*, commander in chief of the Finnish Defense Forces, joined with Adolf Hitler *(left)* of Germany to fight against the Soviet Union from 1941 to 1944.

After its defeat, Finland remained fearful of the Soviet Union. The Soviets seemed ready to join forces with Britain and France. Therefore, Finnish leaders began to think that cooperation with Germany was the best chance to remain free from Soviet rule.

Germany attacked the Soviet Union on June 22, 1941. Thinking German bombing was based in Finland, the Soviets bombed Finnish ports. On June 25, Finland began attacking the Soviet Union. Finns called this second conflict the Continuation War (1941–1944), because it continued the Winter War. Though Finland did not share Nazi Germany's political goals, the two countries fought together against the Soviets.

In September 1944, however, Soviet victories forced Finland to surrender. The war killed eighty-six thousand Finns and disabled fifty-seven thousand more.

The Soviets demanded that the Finns expel 220,000 German troops stationed in northern Finland. In the Lapland War (1944–1945), the third of Finland's wars of this era, the Germans resisted the Finns. As the Germans retreated in the spring, they burned much of the northern countryside. They left Lapland's capital city, Rovaniemi, in ruins.

Caught in the Middle

The Paris Peace Treaty of 1947 ordered Finland to give up Karelia and part of Lapland to the Soviet Union. The USSR also presented the Finns with an enormous bill—$300 million—for war damages.

The Allies accepted the conditions the Soviets placed on Finland. The Finns therefore believed that Western nations would not help Finland if the Soviet Union attacked again. Finnish leaders were concerned. They could see that during World War II the Soviets had taken over Estonia, just across the Gulf of Finland. They did not want the same to happen to their country.

Finland was caught between two opposing alliances—one in Eastern Europe and the other in Western Europe. Eastern Europe came under the control of the Soviet Union. Western Europe remained allied to the United States, the strongest Western power after World War II. The tension between the world's two super-powers and their allies became known as the Cold War (1945–1991). Each side began to stockpile powerful weapons, including nuclear bombs.

The Scandinavian countries of Denmark and Norway joined the North Atlantic Treaty Organization (NATO), a military alliance of Western nations. Sweden remained firmly neutral.

Finland Flourishes

To meet its payments to the USSR, Finland had to change its economy. Through its own efforts, the poor farming country transformed itself into a modern industrial nation. Many rural Finns moved to cities. This movement spurred the rapid growth of Helsinki and other urban areas. People worked hard and prospered.

In 1952 Helsinki hosted the Olympic Games. Finland's athletes came in eighth out of sixty-nine nations. That same year, Armi

Thousands of fans crowd the stands of the Olympic Stadium in Helsinki during the Summer Olympic Games in 1952.

Kuusela of Finland won the first-ever Miss Universe beauty contest. And Finns once again became a force in the world of design.

The death of Soviet dictator Stalin in 1953 brought the first signs of a thaw in the Cold War. In 1955 Finland strengthened its international ties by joining the United Nations and the Nordic Council. The council promotes trade among Nordic states.

Juho Kusti Paasikivi retired in 1956. Urho K. Kekkonen became president. Caught between the East and the West, Kekkonen walked a fine line to keep Finland neutral.

During the 1960s, Finland's economy continued to grow. Culturally, Finland became closer to Western Europe. Rock-and-roll music arrived. People adopted more informal ways of speaking Finnish. The era also saw a revival of Sami culture and pride. Western culture had almost wiped out the traditional worldview and ways of life of the indigenous Sami people of Lapland.

Détente

Finland helped with international efforts to ease Cold War hostilities. The policy of trying to lessen tension was called détente, from a French word meaning "to relax." In 1969 Finland hosted the Strategic Arms Limitation Talks (SALT). These talks between the Soviets and the Americans aimed to reduce the superpowers' buildup of nuclear arms.

In 1975 Helsinki was again the site of an international meeting to reduce Cold War tensions. The conference resulted in thirty-five nations—including the USSR and the United States—signing the Helsinki Accords. In this document, the nations promised to settle differences peacefully and to respect human rights.

The 1970s and 1980s saw a rise in the Finns' concern for the natural environment. The Green movement, which works to protect the environment, became a political party. In this era, the Lutheran church first granted women the right to be ordained as clergy.

While Finland continued to do well, the Soviet Union was crumbling under internal political pressures. Eastern European countries broke away from Soviet control in the late 1980s. The USSR itself broke apart in 1991. Each of the fifteen Soviet republics, including Russia and Estonia, became an independent nation.

New Ties

After the fall of the Soviet Union, Finland's economy suffered. The Soviet Union had been the country's chief trading partner. Finland had especially relied on bartering (swapping) its goods for Soviet oil. The drop in trade hurt Finland's economy. Finns sought new economic ties with western Europe. They also continued to sell goods to Russia and other former Soviet states.

In 1994 Martti Ahtisaari became Finland's president. In October 1994, a majority of Finns voted to join the European Union (EU). This organization pursues economic policies to benefit its members. Nations must have a healthy economy and a democratic society to join the union. The EU accepted Finland's application for membership in 1995.

Finns also celebrated that year when their team won the World Ice Hockey Championships for the first time. The victory was sweeter because they won against Sweden. Though relations between Finland and Sweden were friendly, the memory of Sweden's long rule still lingered in Finland.

The economy continued to grow fast in the 1990s. Ahtisaari only served one term, but he helped reduce high unemployment. The Finnish company Nokia saw the possibilities of the computer and communications revolution. It became the world leader in cell phone technology.

In 1998 Finland adopted the European Union's Natura project. Under this nature conservation plan, Finland protects almost 12 percent of its total land. The next year, Finland began to use the euro—the shared currency of the EU.

NOBEL PEACE PRIZE

In 2008 former Finnish president Martti Ahtisaari won the Nobel Peace Prize (below). As a diplomat, Ahtisaari spent more than thirty years working to resolve conflicts in Namibia, Indonesia, Northern Ireland, Kosovo, and other war-torn regions. He said he believes there is a peaceful solution for every conflict.

▶ The Twenty-First Century

In 2000 Finland swore in its first female president, Tarja Halonen. A longtime politician, she had a reputation for focusing on human rights and social justice. One of her concerns was to help new immigrants and refugees become part of Finnish society. After a group of Finns beat up a Somali youth, Halonen gave a speech warning against racism.

Finnish politician **Tarja Halonen** *(left)* made history when she was elected as the country's first female president in 2000. She was reelected in 2006. This photo shows her with leaders in the fight against climate change at the United Nations Climate Change Conference in 2009.

Anneli Jaatteenmaki became Finland's first female prime minister in 2003. Her term lasted only two months, however. Accusations that she had leaked state secrets forced her to resign. A court cleared her of any wrongdoing the next year. Matti Vanhanen became the next prime minister. In 2006 he held the post of president of the European Council. The council is a group of national leaders from the European Union. President Halonen won a second term in 2006.

In November 2007, a school shooting shocked Finns. A student shot eight people to death and then himself at Jokela high school. Ten months later, a college student's shooting spree ended with eleven people dead, including the shooter. Afterward, the prime minister suggested stricter gun-control laws. Finland has a long tradition of hunting, and its rate of gun ownership is among the highest in the world. But violent crime is low in Finland, and gun murders are rare.

Finns have long been proud of their reputation for honesty. The organization Transparency International ranks countries by their level of corruption, or the misuse of power. For several years, Finland held the rank of least-corrupt nation. In 2008, however, it was revealed that several politicians—including Prime Minister Vanhanen—had not reported large donations of money to their election campaigns. This news led to a growing public distrust of politicians. Parliament quickly established a committee to clean up election funding.

While Finland fell on the corruption index after the scandal, Finland continues to rank high on measurements of prosperity. The country enjoys a high level of prosperity, personal well-being, and quality of life.

Government

Finland is a constitutional republic. That is, the constitution is the source of the nation's laws, and power rests with the people (not a king or queen). All Finns eighteen years and older are eligible to vote. After Finland joined the European Union, a special group revised the constitution. The current constitution took effect in 2000. It moved power away from the president. It invested more power in the prime minister and the parliament, or legislature.

The unicameral (one house) parliament is called the Eduskunta. Voters elect two hundred representatives to serve four-year terms. The parliament elects the prime minister, whom the president then formally appoints. Finland's system of shared representation allows even small political parties to win seats in parliament. Finnish parties have a tradition of joining together to form coalitions. Sometimes the parties in a coalition seem to have opposing political opinions, but their goals are often similar. Working together, small parties can pass laws or change policy.

The president and prime minister share executive power. Voters elect the Finnish president to six-year terms. The president can serve only two terms. With the prime minister, the president also appoints a cabinet called the Council of State. The president is the commander in chief of the armed forces. She or he makes decisions about international affairs, in cooperation with the parliament.

The Finnish judicial branch consists of local courts, regional courts of appeal, and the Supreme Court. The president appoints judges to the Supreme Court. A court must hear a criminal case within eight days of the defendant's arrest.

Finland's six regions are divided into cities, townships, and communes. Elected councils run all levels. The region of Åland has had local self-government since 1921. The president appoints a governor to administer each of the other regions with the help of civil servants (government employees). A Sami Council promotes the concerns of the Sami of Lapland.

Visit www.vgsbooks.com for links to websites with more information about Finland's government and up-to-date news stories about what is happening in Finland.

THE PEOPLE

Finland is the ninth-largest country in Europe, out of fifty-three countries. (Its neighbor Russia is the largest.) With 5.3 million people, however, Finland has almost the sparsest population. Its population density is 40 people per square mile (16 people per sq. km).

Finland's population is growing at 0.9 percent annually—a very slow rate. If this rate continues, the population will reach 5.6 million people by 2025. The average birthrate is 1.8 births per woman. Finns older than 65 account for 17 percent of the population. Children under 15 years make up 17 percent. With fewer young people, the population is less likely to rise. The government is concerned that a dwindling number of adult workers may cause challenges for the economy.

◉ Ethnic Groups

Finland is mostly a uniform society. About 92 percent of Finns are descendants of immigrants who came to the region more than two thousand years ago. Swedish-speaking Finns who trace their ancestry to Sweden make up 5.6 percent of the population. Immigrants, mostly Russians and Estonians, make up about 2.2 percent of the population. Two small ethnic groups—the Roma (formerly called Gypsies) and the Sami (formerly called Lapps)—each account for only 0.1 percent of Finns.

Finland tightly controls the number of immigrants and refugees it allows into the country. Most immigrants come from Russia, Estonia, and Sweden. Parliament sets the quota of refugees (people fleeing conflict or persecution in their home countries) at 750 people per year. The government helps refugees resettle, with language classes and help finding jobs. Refugees from the troubled African nation of Somalia number about 9,000.

Because of Finland's low birthrate, the government is seeking more educated immigrants. It hopes to attract people who will be productive members of society, not burdens on the welfare state. This presents challenges. The country's far northern location, high taxes, and difficult language do not lure many skilled workers. Further, Finland has long been an ethnically unified society. It is not always easy for outsiders to blend in. Estonians, who speak a language close to Finnish, fit into the society fairly well. But many Russian immigrants and others report that they face discrimination in jobs and school.

The Roma have lived in Finland since the 1500s. Numbering about ten thousand, they live mostly in cities. The constitution guarantees the Roma, along with the Sami and other minorities, the right to keep and develop their own language and culture. Though some Roma speak Romani, most speak Finnish.

About nine thousand Sami dwell in northern Finland. (Many more Sami live in Norway, Sweden, and Russia.) They are descendants of some of Finland's earliest peoples and take pride in their ancient culture. Once mainly herders of reindeer, in the twenty-first century, most Sami work in timbering, farming, or tourism.

A small community of eight hundred Tatars also maintains a distinct language and culture in Finland. Originally of Turkish origin, they came to Finland from Russia when Finland was under Russian rule. The Tatars brought their Islamic faith with them.

Gender Equality

Finnish women have long played an active political role in their country. They gained the right to vote and run for election in 1906. Women make up 38 percent of the national legislature. Many Finnish women serve

A Sami family dressed in traditional clothing stands before a traditional Sami house. While the Sami, once called Lapps, are guaranteed rights as full Finnish citizens, they also work hard to preserve their unique cultural heritage.

in public office. Others head trade unions and university departments. Women also make up nearly half of the Finnish workforce. Women in Finland sometimes still earn less than men doing the same work.

The military remains another area of difference between the treatment of men and women. The law requires all Finnish men eighteen or older to serve six months in the military. They may choose to serve twelve months of civilian (nonarmed) service instead. Women may enter the military if they want, but the law does not require them to join. Few women choose to join.

Health and Social Welfare

Finland is a welfare state—that is, a country whose government guarantees the basic needs of all its citizens. Finns choose to pay high taxes to fund social-welfare programs. The government spends about one-third of its budget on providing free or low-cost public services. These include education, low-cost health care, and old age and disability pensions. The government pays for new mothers and fathers to take time off work. It makes monthly payments to families with children who are younger than seventeen years old. Local governments run day-care centers for pre-school children whose parents work outside the home.

The average number of Finnish babies who die before their first birthday is 2.7 deaths per 1,000 births. The world average is 49 deaths per 1,000 babies.

Local governments also help elderly people to stay in their homes. Assistance is available for cleaning, cooking, shopping, and

Two nurses prepare an intravenous bag for a patient. Health care in Finland is provided by the government to all Finns.

PREVENTING SUICIDE

Few societies in Europe changed as rapidly as Finland did after World War II. The quick switch from a traditional farming life to modern city life brought improvements. But many people struggled to adapt to the huge changes in their way of life. Depression and suicide rates began to rise alarmingly in the 1960s. By 1991 Finland led the world in the number of teen suicides. And it was in the top three nations for suicides among all ages. Faced with these grim facts, the Finnish government began to spend money on mental health programs. Recognition, prevention, and treatment of depression greatly increased. As a result, deaths by suicide dropped 40 percent. In the twenty-first century, Finland's rate of suicide is about the same as France's.

transportation. Special centers provide information and social activities for the elderly.

The government gives housing allowances to students, to pensioners, and to families with children. Families with below-average incomes are eligible for long-term loans with low interest rates from the government. Many of the borrowers use the money to buy or build their own homes.

The government operates most hospitals, where patients pay about 13 percent of their costs. Visits to the doctor and most medications are free or low-cost. Finland has some of the best health statistics in the world. Life expectancy is 79 years overall (83 years for women and 76 for men). The percent of adults infected with HIV/AIDS is less than 0.1.

Finns struggle with the same health issues that citizens of other wealthy nations do. Cancer, heart disease, unhealthy lifestyles, poor stress management, and cigarette smoking all take their toll. Alcoholism rates are high in Finland. Alcohol-related death is the leading cause of early death for Finnish men. It is the second-largest cause of death for women in the same age group.

Education

Finland is a highly educated society. The constitution guarantees all Finns the right to basic education, free of charge. The country spends 6.4 percent of its national income on education. This is a very high rate, compared to most of the world. The government reports a 100 percent rate of literacy, or the ability to read and write a basic sentence.

In grades one through six, students study environmental studies, history, math, and physical education. In grades seven through nine, students also take classes in religion, geography, and the arts. In addition, each student begins courses in a second language, in chemistry, in physics, and in home economics. All students must study Swedish, and most students also study English.

After primary school, most young Finns advance to one of two types of secondary schools. The three-year senior secondary school emphasizes academic education. Graduating students must take a national examination to qualify for university entrance.

The other type of secondary school offers vocational education. Students choose from about twenty-five subjects and then pick either a long or a short program. During the first year, all students take general studies. In the second year, they begin to specialize. Short programs, which last for one or two years, lead to entry-level jobs. Long courses last three or four years. They prepare students for careers as supervisors.

Finland's largest postsecondary school is the University of Helsinki. The cities of Turku, Tampere, Oulu, and Jyväskylä each have universities. About 1,600 students study music at Finland's music university, the Sibelius Academy in Helsinki. The rate of Finns studying music is higher than in any other country. The state owns all of Finland's universities. Taxes pay for students' tuition. Students can apply to the government for grants and low-interest loans to pay their living expenses.

CHILDREN ARE PEOPLE TOO

The Finnish constitution singles out children and their rights. Chapter 2 of the constitution states that everyone is equal before the law. Section 6 specifically mentions children: "Children shall be treated equally and as individuals and they shall be allowed to influence matters pertaining to themselves to a degree corresponding to their level of development."

A teacher hands out supplies to her second-grade students in an elementary school in Vaasa, Finland.

Language

Finland has two official languages—Finnish and Swedish. About 91 percent of Finland's people speak Finnish as their first language. Swedish is the mother tongue of almost 6 percent of the population. A little more than 3 percent speak a Sami language, Romani, Russian, or other language. All students must learn Swedish or Finnish languages in school.

Finnish words contain many vowels and double consonants. The alphabet does not include the letters *b*, *c*, *f*, *w*, *x*, or *z*. An umlaut, or two dots, above *a* and *o* changes their sound. An *ä* sounds like the *a* in "bat." An *ö* sounds like the *e* in "her." Words are often quite long. The Finnish language has borrowed many words from Swedish.

Finnish and Swedish are not related. Finnish belongs to the Finno-Ugric group along with languages spoken in Estonia, Hungary, Lapland, and parts of Russia. This language group originated in eastern and northern Europe. Swedish, on the other hand, is an Indo-European tongue. It is related to the languages in the rest of Europe, including English.

Finnish is a unique language. It is related to Hungarian, but only distantly. Speakers of closely related languages, such as Swedish and Danish, can understand one another with a little effort. But Finns and Hungarians can't. Almost the only words their languages have in common are about fishing. A language scholar came up with only one sentence Finns and Hungarians could both understand: "The living fish swims in the water."

The Finnish constitution recognizes the Sami and Roma languages. Three Sami languages are spoken in Finland. These tongues are related to Finnish. Fewer than two thousand people in Finland claim Sami as their first language. About half the Finnish Sami can speak Sami as their second language. People are concerned the Sami languages may die out. Some parents send their children to "language nests," or programs where they learn the language at a young age.

Religion

Religion does not play a large role in Finland's public life. Most Finns consider religion a private matter. Only about 4 percent say they attend religious services weekly. This is one of the lowest rates in the world.

About 83 percent of the Finnish people belong to the Evangelical Lutheran Church. Most Lutherans attend church for baptism, confirmation, marriage, and funerals. The Orthodox Church is the

People attend a wedding at **Porvoo Cathedral** in Porvoo, Finland.

country's second traditional church. Members make up a little more than 1 percent of the population, mostly in eastern Finland. The government collects taxes to support those two churches. People who are not Lutheran or Orthodox do not have to pay the religious taxes. More than 15 percent of people in Finland claim no religious affiliation.

Another 1 percent of Finns practice Pentecostal, Roman Catholic, Islamic, or Jewish faiths. Laestadians are Finnish Christian evangelists. They hold a large four-day spiritual revival meeting in a different location in Finland each summer. Islam came to the Grand Duchy of Finland with the Tatars in the 1800s. Recent immigrants from various countries in the Islamic world have raised the number of Muslims to between 10,000 and 20,000. Finnish Jews number about 1,300, mostly of Russian origin.

Christianity almost totally replaced the traditional Sami religion. A Sami cultural revival of the 1960s brought the religion to light again. In this belief system, there are three worlds. They are the earthly world of the living, a spiritual world where souls go after death, and an upper world of gods. A shaman is a special holy person whose soul can travel between all three worlds. The Sami shaman uses a special drum and chants *yoiks*, or traditional songs, to reach the trance state to make such soul journeys. In the past, the shaman provided advice about reindeer herding as well as medical and spiritual help to the community.

 Visit www.vgsbooks.com for links to websites to learn more about the Finnish language and hear people speaking in Finnish.

CULTURAL LIFE

Finland's cultural traditions run deep and wide. Finnish music ranges from the romantic classical music of Jean Sibelius to the heavy metal songs of Nightwish. Architects and designers are known for bold designs employing natural materials. Finns have been on skis for thousands of years, and the country produces more than their share of world-class athletes. The ancient legends of Finland's national epic the *Kalevala* continue to inspire artists, musicians, and writers.

Young Finns, however, also grew up watching U.S. television shows and movies and using the Internet. In the twenty-first century, Finns make the most of the global revolution in technology. Finland's culture draws on the past as it creates the future.

◉ Literature

The first Finnish-language book appeared in 1543. It was an ABC book published by Bishop Mikael Agricola. He also translated the Bible into Finnish and is known as the father of Finnish literature.

But for hundreds of years, most Finnish authors wrote in Swedish. After Finland became part of Russia in 1808, Finns took an increasing pride in their own language and legends.

Elias Lönnrot helped forge a national identity for Finns when he gathered ancient folktales and myths in Karelia. In 1835 he published the *Kalevala*—a collection of stories based on the tales. Johan Ludvig Runeberg was a Swedish-speaking Finn. His patriotic poetry expressed the Finnish yearning for independence.

Finnish writers often related the tragic fate of people who cannot control the larger forces around them. Forests and nature are common settings. Aleksis Kivi set the standard for Finnish-language novels and plays. With humor and realism, his novel, *Seven Brothers*, portrays the lives of seven backwoods brothers. Folklore influenced the poetry of Eino Leino. Sometimes lighthearted, sometimes dark and heroic, his poetry is still quoted by Finns. In 1939 Frans Eemil Sillanpää received the Nobel Prize in Literature for *Nuorena nukkunut* (*Fallen Asleep While*

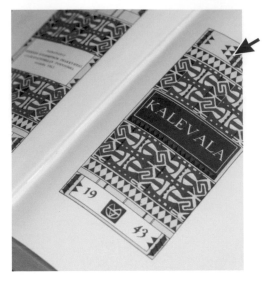

Young), his tragic novel about a rural girl named Silja. Väinö Linna based his powerful novel *The Unknown Soldier* on his experiences in the Continuation War. This antiwar tale has twice been made into movies.

Kirsi Kunnas is one of Finland's best-loved children's poets. Sweet but strange hippolike creatures called Moomin are the creation of author-illustrator Tove Jansson. The Finnish airline FinnAir even flies a plane decorated with Moomin characters.

In modern times, Finns read more books than citizens of most other countries. The long winter nights may help explain this national pastime. Readers have many Finnish authors to choose from. Nils-Aslak Valkeapää was a Sami author who often wrote in Finnish. Kjell Westö is one of Finland's favorite dramatic writers. His novel *Lang* (2006) follows a talk-show host who gets caught up in a dangerous love affair. Ilkka Remes, Matti Rönkä, and Leena Lehtolainen are best-selling authors of crime and detective novels. Veijo Baltzar is a Finn of Roma background. He writes novels about the little known Roma way of life. Sofi Oksanen is an up-and-coming author. Her 2008 novel *Puhdistus* (*Purge*) concerns the horrors Estonian women have endured.

In 2008 the Finnish magazine *Books from Finland* went online. Its English-language website presents writing from and about Finland. Readers can also find excerpts of novels and interviews with many authors there.

◉ Film

The 1955 film *The Unknown Soldier* is the most successful Finnish film to date. Based on an antiwar novel, this story

This Finnish postage stamp features one of Tove Jansson's well-known creatures, the **Moomin.**

of soldiers in the Continuation War attracted a huge audience. It plays every year on television on December 6, Finland's Independence Day.

Mika Kaurismäki's first film *The Liar* (1980) marked the beginning of a wave of low-budget independent films. Johnny Depp appeared in Kaurismäki's 1998 comedy *L.A. Without a Map*. Mika's brother Aki Kaurismäki is one of Finland's best-known moviemakers. His film *The Man Without a Past* takes a sympathetic and sometimes funny look at the plight of people who fall through the welfare net of Finnish society. It competed for the 2003 Academy Awards for Best Foreign Language Film. Director Klaus Härö's film *Mother of Mine* was Finland's entry in the 2005 Academy Awards. It tells the story of a boy whose mother sends him to Sweden for safety during the Continuation War. In 2008 *The Home of the Dark Butterflies* told a boy's traumatic coming-of-age story. It is based on a novel by Leena Lander.

Finnish director Renny Harlin works in Hollywood making blockbuster action movies. He often includes a nod to his homeland in films he directs. You can hear Sibelius's *Finlandia*, for instance, at the end of *Die Hard 2*.

Music

Finland's popular music scene ranges from the Finnish tango to heavy metal. Traditional Sami songs are part of the country's folk music heritage. Classical music includes orchestra conductors and opera singers.

Heavy metal and hard rock music is very popular in Finland. Metal fans come to Helsinki every summer for the Tuska (Agony) Open Air Metal Festival. Nightwish is one of the country's most famous

Nightwish, one of Finland's most popular heavy metal bands, has become famous around the world.

metal bands. With a powerful female lead singer and dark lyrics, their albums have sold more than 5 million copies worldwide. The metal band Children of Bodom also enjoys international fame. The band Lordi performed "Hard Rock Hallelujah" to win the Eurovision Song Contest in 2006. Apocalyptica became the first Finnish band to reach no. 1 on the U.S. *Billboard* rock chart, with their haunting 2008 single, "I Don't Care." They record with a variety of singers, including Ville Valo, frontman for the Finnish rock band HIM.

Rap artists like Cheek and Pikku G mostly rap in Finnish. The hip-hop group Fintelligens wrote the smash-hit theme song to Ice Hockey World Championships in 2003. Rapper Elastinen's cool music videos are popular with young people.

The Finnish tango is popular among older Finns. Every summer, the town of Seinäjoki holds a tango festival and crowns a tango queen and king. Known as the Frank Sinatra of Finland, tango singer Olavi Virta recorded more than six hundred songs in the mid-twentieth century. Finnish tango crosses over into a style of sweetly sad pop music called *schlager*. Jari Sillanpää, a tango king from the 1990s, is a popular schlager singer.

Finnish folk music is part of the global music scene known as World Music. Bands such as Frigg create modern music based on traditional songs. Ancient Finnish instruments include a plucked-string zither called the *kantele*. Its bell-like sounds accompany readings of *Kalevala* legends.

Jean Sibelius (1865–1957) is Finland's most famous classical composer. Finnish landscapes and folk melodies inspired his orchestral music. *Finlandia* is Sibelius's best-

THE SAMI YOIK

The *yoik*, also spelled *joik*, is a style of Sami song. The yoiker may or may not use words. Yoiks sound somewhat like chanting, and sometimes a drum accompanies the singer. The vocalizations carry the spiritual essence of a person or place. The structure of the yoik reflects the Sami worldview: a circle of nature, with no beginning and no end.

Yoiking had almost died out by the 1960s. In that decade, Nils-Aslak Valkeapää, born into a reindeer-herding family, began recording and performing yoiks. He brought the style into the world music scene. Wimme Saari is a leading modern Sami musician. Some Sami musicians blend yoiking with other music styles. Mari Boine is another popular Sami singer. She adds jazz and rock elements to yoik. "Folk metal" incorporates heavy metal with folk music. The Finnish band Shaman drew on Sami music to create yoik metal.

known work. In the twenty-first century, classical musicians include composer and conductor Esa-Pekka Salonen. Conductor Osmo Vänskä became the Minnesota Orchestra's music director in 2003.

Finland's tradition of great opera singers dates to the early 1900s, when the soprano Aino Ackte was an international star. She founded the Savonlinna Opera Festival. This annual event still draws opera lovers from all over. In the twenty-first century, Karita Mattila's electrifying soprano voice has made her a superstar.

Jean Sibelius

▶ Art and Design

Finnish architecture and design has drawn praise since it came to the world's attention at the 1900 Paris World's Fair. Architect Eliel Saarinen's firm designed the Finnish Pavilion at the fair. Akseli Gallen-Kallela displayed textile designs and richly colored paintings, some based on the *Kalevala*.

In the mid-twentieth century, Finnish designers were central to Scandinavian modernism. They believed that beautiful, well-made

This car is painted in the hip poppy pattern of Marimekko, a Finnish textile and clothing design company that has strongly influenced modern Finnish fashion.

objects should be available to everyone. The design had a modern streamlined look but employed old-fashioned materials such as blonde (light-colored) wood and natural fibers. One of the biggest names in Scandinavian modernism was Alvar Aalto. In 1937 Aalto created a glass vase with a wavy outline, like the shoreline of a Finnish lake. It became a symbol of Nordic design.

Modern Finnish architects include Raimo and Raili Pietilä. They designed the Finnish president's residence and the Tampere city library. Harri Koskinen is a modern designer whose furniture and household objects win international awards.

Modern painters use a variety of styles. Kaj Stenvall paints a cartoon duck into his otherwise traditional-looking paintings. It ends up in troubling—and sometimes amusing—situations. Kristiina Uusitalo captures images of nature using some Asian painting techniques. For instance, her sweeping brushwork captures the movement of wind on water.

Finland's craftspeople manufacture pottery, glassware, furniture, and textiles. Folk art influences artist Oiva Toikka's glass sculptures and objects, including his birds made of colorful swirling glass.

In the past, Sami people relied on being able to read signs and symbols in nature to survive. Sami artists often used symbols to represent the natural world—the energy of the sun, the growth of forests. Many modern Sami artists include traditional symbols in nontraditional art forms.

Sports and Recreation

Finns participate in sports year-round. Cross-country skiing is the favorite national sport. Canoeing, rowing, swimming, and sailing on one of Finland's many lakes are also popular. Many Finnish families own summerhouses near water.

The sauna is a cornerstone of Finnish life. It is a special bathhouse or small room where water is poured over hot stones to produce steam. The heat and steam relax muscles and clean the skin through sweating. After a while, the sauna users plunge into a cold pool, a lake, or a shower. According to the Finnish Tourist Board, Finland counts 750,000 boats, 465,000 summer cottages, and 1.8 million saunas—about one sauna for every three people.

Ice hockey tops the country's spectator sports. Many Finns play ice hockey and soccer. Among

Finland hosts the Wife-Carrying World Championships in Sonkajärvi each July. Men carry a female teammate through an obstacle course. Though Finland started this event (as a joke), the country lost to Estonia for ten years in a row. In 2009 a Finnish couple finally won the event again.

Almost every family in Finland has its own **sauna.** For Finns the sauna is an important part of healthy living because of its ability to cleanse the body and skin.

Finland's popular team sports are a form of ice hockey called *bandy* and *pesäpallo*, which resembles baseball.

Finnish athletes in track-and-field events and skiing have done especially well in world competitions. Long-distance runners—including Paavo Nurmi and Ville Ritola—won many Olympic medals during their careers. Nurmi was nicknamed the Flying Finn for his speed and stamina on the track.

Competitive skiing takes several forms. Kalle Palander and Tanja Poutiainen are top Alpine, or downhill, ski racers. Palander specializes in the slalom, or skiing down a twisty course marked by poles. Ski jumping is a daredevil sport, and Finns are also among its top competitors. Matti Nykänen and Toni Nicminen both won Olympic gold medals in ski-jumping events. Cross-country skiing in Finland suffered from doping scandals at the 2001 Nordic World Ski Championships. Six Finnish cross-country skiers tested positive for performance enhancing drugs. After a two-year suspension for doping, Virpi Kuitunen went on to earn a bronze medal in the women's team sprint at the 2006 Winter Olympics in Turin, Italy.

Many Finns follow Formula 1 (F1) car racing on television. F1 cars race at speeds up to 220 miles (354 km) per hour. The country has produced more Formula 1 world champions per capita than anywhere else. In 2007 Kimi Räikkönen became the third Finn to win the World Driver's Champion. Räikkönen earned his nickname, Iceman, for

Kimi Räikkönen races in the Abu Dhabi Formula 1 Grand Prix in 2009. Formula 1 is a popular sport for Finns to watch on television.

keeping his cool under pressure. A lot of drivers learned their skills driving go-karts, a very popular pastime among Finnish youth. Finnish drivers also boast an impressive six world championships in rallying. This motorsport doesn't take place on racetracks but from point to point on roads.

▶ Holidays

Most national Finnish holidays have Christian origins. Some traditions carry over from the time when Finns worshiped Earth spirits. For instance, long ago, people lit bonfires to frighten off evil spirits they believed haunted Finland in the spring. In modern times, bonfires still dot the countryside around the Christian holiday of Easter.

Finns celebrate Vappu, or May Day, with enthusiasm. Parades, fairs, and concerts mark this first day of May. Juhannus, or Midsummer Day, falls on or near June 24. Finns celebrate with bonfires and rites once believed to bring fertility and good harvests. At midsummer festivals, Finnish families practice old rituals that foretell the future. For example, a girl may place certain herbs under her pillow to make her dream of her future husband.

Independence Day on December 6 commemorates the declaration of independence from Russia in 1917. The president hosts a glamorous party every year, but the event is not a major public holiday.

Christmas is the most celebrated holiday of the year for most Finns. Cooks prepare special foods, including ham, rice pudding, and Christmas pies. Images of Joulupukki (Christmas goat) appear everywhere during the Christmas season. This goat has evolved into human form as the Finnish version of Santa Claus.

 Visit www.vgsbooks.com for links to websites with additional information about holidays and traditions in Finland as well as more about the music, the design, and the sports that Finnish people enjoy.

Food

Breakfast in Finland often consists of an open-faced sandwich topped with slices of cold meats, cheese, and cucumbers and other vegetables. Cereal with yogurt or another sour milk dish called *viili* is common breakfast fare too. Lunch is often the main meal of the day. A common late-afternoon treat is the Finnish cinnamon roll. Dinner is usually a light meal, such as pea soup. Wild mushrooms from Finland's forests also make a flavorful soup.

Santa Claus is called Joulupukki in Finland, which means "Yule goat" or "Yule buck." Joulupukki is said to live in the Korvatunturi Mountains of Lapland.

CINNAMON ROLLS (KORVAPUUSTIT)

These rolls smell like home to Finns. Making them takes some time, but they are worth it. You can substitute frozen bread dough, following package directions, and start with Step 6.

Dough

1 cup milk

½ cup sugar

1 packet yeast

2 eggs, beaten

½ cup (1 stick) butter, melted

1 teaspoon salt

1 teaspoon cardamom

4 plus 1 cups flour

Filling

¼ cup (½ stick) butter, soft

1 tablespoon cinnamon

3 tablespoons sugar

Topping

1 egg, beaten

1 to 2 tablespoons sugar

1. Heat milk to warm (not hot). In a large bowl, stir sugar and yeast into milk. Let sit about 5 minutes, until the yeast dissolves.
2. Stir 2 beaten eggs and melted butter into milk.
3. Add salt and cardamom to 4 cups flour. Gradually add the flour to the yeast and milk.
4. Sprinkle flour on a flat surface. Put dough ball on it. With the heels of your hands, knead (push and turn) 1 cup flour into the dough, a little at a time. Knead for 8 minutes, until smooth.
5. Put dough in bowl, and cover with a kitchen towel. Let dough rise in a warm place until double in size, about 1 hour.
6. Turn dough onto a floured surface. With a rolling pin, roll dough into a thin, rectangular sheet. Spread the soft butter all over the sheet. Mix cinnamon and sugar, and evenly sprinkle on dough.
7. Tightly roll the sheet of dough into a log, starting from the longer side. Cut the log, on an angle, into 14 triangle-shaped wedges. Turn each wedge so it sits on the wide end of the triangle. Press the center point down with your finger, so the swirly cut edges bulge out.
8. Place rolls on a cookie sheet. Let sit for 30 minutes. Then brush the tops with beaten egg, and sprinkle with sugar.
9. Bake in 425°F oven, for 15 minutes, or until golden brown. Serve warm.

Makes 14 rolls

You can find **korvapuustit, the traditional Finnish cinnamon roll,** in just about every bakery and café in Finland.

Finnish cuisine relies on the flavors of natural ingredients rather than a lot of spices. Vegetables include root crops such as red beets, turnips, and potatoes. There are dozens of kinds of bread, including crisp cracker breads. Dark Finnish rye bread is especially good with the country's cheeses. Beef, pork, and fish are the staple meats. They may appear as sausages or Finnish meatballs. Cooks prepare fish in many ways, such as fish soup, fish pie, smoked salmon, and pickled herring. Hunters bring home game meats such as duck, pheasants, rabbits, and elk.

People gather wild strawberries and other berries in summer. Lingonberries are small, tart red berries, like cranberries. Sweetened, they are often served with meats. Cloudberries look like golden yellow raspberries. The tart berries are made into jams and liqueurs, or they are eaten with a special cheese. Blueberry soup or pie is a traditional Finnish dessert.

Many traditional dishes come from the time when most Finns led rural lives. Some examples are reindeer with lingonberries, duck with forest mushrooms, and roasted trout or crayfish fresh from a lake. The Karelian pasty, or stuffed pie, is a regional specialty. Either sweet or savory, it is popular all over the country.

Coffee and milk are everyday beverages. Finns drink coffee all day long, and major cities have dozens of cafés. Adults often drink liqueurs and brandies made from locally grown fruits.

Finns drink more coffee than any other people in the world—about 24 pounds (11 kilograms) per person every year. That's about five cups a day, twice the amount of coffee the average Italian drinks.

THE ECONOMY

Finland is a modern, highly industrialized society. Finland joined the European Union in 1995 and engages in free trade with other member nations. Finland's average earnings per person are $34,550. This is similar to the averages in France and Germany. Timber industries are still important, but information and communication industries are key to Finland's economy. Finland is a world leader in cell phone and other high-tech products. A global economic slowdown began to put a brake on Finland's growth in 2008. But Finland's economy remains one of the strongest in the European Union. Finns are also proud of their reputation for honesty in business.

◉ Services

Services provide 65 percent of Finland's gross domestic product (GDP, the value of the goods and services a country produces in one year). Jobs in this sector provide services rather than producing goods. Almost 70 percent of Finns work in service jobs such as banking and business

services, and transportation and communication work. Government public service jobs employ the largest number of Finnish workers. These include work in education, health care, and administration.

Tourism adds about $4 million to Finland's GDP every year. Finland's magnificent scenery is its main attraction for visitors. They come to enjoy spas, ski resorts, hiking, boating, and viewing the northern lights. The largest numbers of tourists come from Sweden, Germany, Russia, and the United Kingdom.

▶ Industry

Industry accounts for 32 percent of Finland's GDP. It includes manufacturing, mining, power, and the building trades. This sector employs about 25 percent of the workforce.

Finland's large wood and paper industries benefit from the country's abundant stocks of good-quality timber. Wood and pulp enterprises are among the nation's leading exports. About 80 percent of the products

CRUISE SHIP CONSTRUCTION

The world's largest cruise ship the *Oasis of the Sea* set sail from Finland on her maiden voyage in late 2009. Hundreds of workers spent two and a half years constructing the $1.5 billion vessel at a shipyard in Turku. They built the ship in cubes and then put them together like Lego building bricks. Engineers took environmental considerations into account in designing the ship. It doesn't dump sewage into the sea, it recycles its wastewater, and it uses 25 percent less power than smaller cruise ships. Complete with an open-air Central Park, the *Oasis* is home to twelve thousand live plants. It holds 6,300 passengers and 2,100 crew. The Norwegian-U.S. company Royal Caribbean owns the ship.

from wood and paper mills are sold abroad, mostly to western Europe.

The nation earns considerable income from manufacturing metal goods, heavy machinery, and vehicles such as ships. Finland's main metal products are made of copper and high-technology steels. The principal engineered goods are electronic and optical equipment, including cell phones. Factories also make agricultural and forestry machines, cranes and lifts, oil rigs, and electrical and papermaking equipment. Finnish shipbuilding yards construct specialized ships such as icebreakers and passenger vehicles.

High-quality design and precise crafting have made Finnish consumer goods popular throughout the world. Quality goods include textiles, clothing, furniture, ceramics, and glassware. Other Finnish manufactured products include

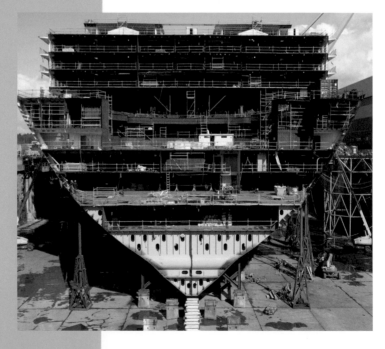

The *Oasis of the Sea* was under construction in Turku, Finland, from 2007 to 2009.

foodstuffs, alcoholic beverages, and tobacco. Finland's chemical industries refine oil and manufacture pharmaceuticals and fertilizers.

Finland depends largely on imported raw materials, fuels, and some foreign-made parts to make many of its engineered products. Investors from abroad stimulate Finnish economic growth both by lending money to Finnish companies and by building plants in Finland.

Mining and Energy

Mining and quarrying are a small part of the industrial sector. Gold is the main mineral export. Finns mine iron ore, copper, lead, zinc, cobalt, and tin in east central Finland. Nickel and lead also exist. Supplies of titanium and vanadium are among the country's minerals used to make high-grade steel. Finland's nonmetallic minerals include sulfur, graphite, granite, and limestone. The Finnish ceramics industry uses the nation's stock of feldspar, quartz, and clay.

Finland is one of the largest consumers of power, per person, in the world. The country holds no oil of its own. To help meet the demand, the country operates four nuclear power plants. Domestic energy sources also include hydroelectric power and wood waste from the forestry industry. Peat—decayed vegetation packed down and layered in bogs—is another Finnish fuel. Finns cut peat into blocks, dry them, and then burn them like wood. Peat is so plentiful it even fuels some power plants. Foreign oil meets about 40 percent of the country's requirements. Finland also imports nuclear power, coal, and natural gas to cover the remaining demand.

Agriculture

Agriculture brings in 3 percent of Finland's GDP. Only about 5 percent of Finns work in this sector, which includes farming, fishing, and forestry.

Forestry is the most important part of the agricultural sector. Forests are vital to the health of Finland's economy. Private individuals or families own about 60 percent of the timberlands. The government holds title to about 30 percent, and corporations control the remainder. The country's tree stocks consist chiefly of pine, spruce, and birch. Aspen and alder are also common.

Finns use pine tar to water-proof boats, to mix in soaps and shampoos, and also as a flavoring for food and sweets. One can find pine tar liquor, pine tar sauces for meat and fish, and even pine tar candy.

Agriculture and forestry are closely linked in Finland. Farmers traditionally earn money by working as loggers in the winter months.

Almost 90 percent of Finnish farms are still small and family run. Small farms and the country's short growing season keep agricultural productivity in Finland relatively low. The output of agricultural goods has increased very little since the 1960s. Many families have abandoned rural areas for better opportunities in cities. The number of farmers has dropped as new machinery and methods have replaced the need for farm laborers. Finns who remain on their farms often rely on the help of subsidies (payments from the government).

Finland is self-sufficient in dairy products, eggs, and meat. But the nation imports large amounts of fruits, vegetables, and grain. Dairy and livestock products account for most of the country's agricultural output. Farmers specialize in dairy and beef cattle, pigs, and chickens. The chief crops are barley, oats, and sugar beets. Other crops include hay, wheat, rye, oilseed plants, and potatoes.

Commercial fishing fleets operate from Turku and the Åland Islands. Boats bring in large hauls of Baltic herring. This is the most popular saltwater fish in Finland. The Baltic Sea's high level of pollution endangers the local herring catch. The country's lakes provide ample sportfishing. Freshwater fish in Finland include whitefish, salmon, perch, and pike.

Turnip rape is grown as an oilseed plant in Finland. The Baltic herring is the most important fish in Finland, both as a source of income and food for the people and as prey for larger animals in the Baltic Sea.

High-Tech and Nokia

Finland is a world leader in technology. The country leads the field in science, math, and engineering education. Its patents and earnings from technology are also ahead of the pack.

Nokia is Finland's leading high-tech company, and the country's biggest company of any kind. Nokia offered its first cell phone in 1982. In 1997 construction was completed on Nokia House, the company's ultramodern head office in Espoo.

In 1982 Nokia introduced one of the world's first cordless, handheld phones. The Mobira Senator, a car phone, weighed 22 pounds (10 kg).

The company produces 40 percent of all cell phones sold in the world. Nokia continues to research and develop new products and services that bring together the Internet and mobile communications. New mini-laptops called booklets came out in 2009. With employees worldwide, the company uses English as its official language.

Nokia is a huge force in Finland's economy. It earns $35 billion dollars a year—about the size of the Finnish government's entire budget. About twenty-two thousand Finns work for Nokia and voted it the best employer in the country.

With 92 percent of households owning at least one cell phone, Finland leads the world in cell-phone ownership. Finns provide only 1.5 percent of Nokia's sales, but almost everyone in the country owns a Nokia cell phone, even children. More cell phones are in use than landlines.

Communications and Media

Finland's modern communications system provides excellent service. In a country of 5.3 million people, there are 6.8 million cell

A group of teenagers in the west coast town of Vaasa talk on their cell phones. Most people in Finland own cell phones.

phones and 1.7 million landlines in use. Satellites and cables under the Baltic Sea provide international connections. Finland is a leading country in Internet use. More than 3.7 million Finns are Internet users. The Finnish government passed a law making broadband internet access a legal right in 2009, effective in July 2010.

Raha, the Finnish word for "money," originally referred to squirrel skins. It comes from ancient times when Finns traded furs for Roman metal goods and jewelry.

Finland's constitution guarantees freedom of speech. All the country's 120 television stations broadcast signals digitally. More than 60 radio stations offer news, sports, and music. Ever-growing numbers of Finns read the paper online.

Foreign Trade

Finland has a healthy balance of trade. It exports, or sells to other countries, more than it imports, or buys. High-tech exports, including cell phones and other electronics products lead the nation's exports. Other goods include machinery, metals and metal products, and chemicals. From its forests, Finland exports timber, paper, and pulp. Ships, clothing, and footwear are among its trade goods. Finland sells mainly to the European Union (especially Germany), Russia, Sweden, and the United States.

Finland produces little oil and no natural gas. It depends on imported petroleum products, such as gasoline. Because of the country's harsh climate and limited farmland, it must buy some of its food from abroad. It also buys raw materials, machinery, and some parts to make manufactured goods. Consumer goods such as cars and clothes account for a large amount of imports. The European Union, Russia, and Sweden are Finland's main import partners. It also buys goods from China.

Visit www.vgsbooks.com for links to websites with additional information about Finland's economy and the products it produces.

Transportation

Finland's sparse population over large distances and its severe climate pose transportation challenges. Ports, for example, require a large fleet of icebreakers to keep shipping lanes open during the winter. Snowplows keep streets clear of snow. Repairing roads from winter damage is expensive.

The country maintains a total of 48,554 miles (78,141 km) of roads. Paved roads account for 31,636 miles (50,914 km), including 435 miles

During the winter in Finland, **specially designed ships called icebreakers** clear the ice in waterways. This ship is clearing ice in the Gulf of Bothnia in northern Finland.

(700 km) of expressways.

Finland has an extensive railway network. Trains travel over 3,600 miles (5,794 km) of track. More than half the railways run on electric power. Helsinki operates an underground railway.

Finland's many waterways allow for 4,873 miles (7,842 km) of boat travel. Canals link rivers and lakes for cargo and passenger vessels and the transport of timber. Finland's main seaports for shipping are Kotka and Helsinki.

Airplanes are another common means of getting around Finland. The country has 148 airports, and 75 of them have paved runways. The main international airport is near Helsinki. The country's main international carrier is FinnAir. It offers flights inside Finland, to European cities, and to ten cities farther abroad, including the United States and Japan.

The Future

Finland faces several challenges. The global economic downturn that began in 2008 drove Finland's unemployment rate up. The government had to cut some public services, including some health-care benefits. Experts expect the economy to recover gradually. The aging of Finland's workforce is a long-term concern. A lack of young people to take the place of retiring workers could lead to a less productive economy. Finland's social welfare system costs a lot of money, and it relies on Finnish workers paying high taxes. But Finns have a record of surviving and developing in the face of challenges. Their economy is as good as or better than the rest of the European Union. The country manages to balance a good business environment while protecting its natural environment. Finns are known for their honesty, hard work, and stable law and order. With a well-educated population, Finland is well positioned to face its challenges.

CA. 8000 B.C.	People first arrive in Finland, at the end of the last ice age. They hunted and fished for food.
CA. 3500 B.C.	Finno-Ugric nomads move into Finland from north and central Russia. Their language will become modern Finnish.
CA. 200 B.C.	Iron Age Finnish peoples have learned to make iron tools and weapons. In this era, Germanic groups called the boat-axe peoples reach Finland from northern Europe.
A.D. 97	The Roman historian Tacitus describes a people he called Fenni, probably the ancestors of modern Finns.
800	Fleets of Swedish adventurers called Vikings come to Finland.
1155	King Erik of Sweden first tries to force the Roman Catholic faith on Finland, beginning almost seven hundred years of Swedish rule of Finland.
1543	Mikael Agricola publishes the first Finnish-language book, an ABC book.
1640	Per Brahe establishes Finland's first university, at Turku.
1672	Swedish king Karl XI strengthened Finland's ties to Swedish culture and language. He also orders that all Finns should learn to read and write.
1696–1697	Hunger and disease kill one-third of Finland's population.
1700–1721	Sweden and Russia battle each other for control of northern Europe during the Great Northern War. Finns suffer Russian occupation.
1743	Sweden and Russia agree to the Peace of Turku. Most of Finland remains part of Sweden, but Russia gains part of eastern Finland.
1808	Russia and Sweden begin the Finnish War. The next year, Russia gains full control of Finland, ending Sweden's long rule.
1835	Elias Lönnrot publishes the *Kalevala*, his collection of ancient Finnish folktales. The book inspires Finns to promote their own culture.
1848	A gathering of nationalistic students sing "Vårt land" (Our Country), and the song becomes Finland's national anthem.
1863	Johan Vilhelm Snellman and others force the government to use Finnish as well as the traditional Swedish.
1900	Finnish artists gain praise at the Paris World's Fair.
1906	Finnish women gain the right to vote and hold political office.
1917	The Finnish parliament (the Eduskunta) declares Finland's independence.

1918   From January until May, Finns fight the Civil War. Led by
Carl Mannerheim, the White faction wins and establishes
the Republic of Finland.

1920   Runner Paavo Nurmi—nicknamed the Flying Finn—sets world records
at the Olympic Games.

1937   Alvar Aalto's wavy-edged glass vase becomes a symbol of Nordic design.

1939   Frans Eemil Sillanpää wins the Nobel Prize in Literature. The Soviet Union
attacks Finland, and Finns fight the Winter War.

1941   Finland again goes to war with the Soviet Union in the Continuation War.

1945   Finland drives German troops out of Lapland in the Lapland War. Author-illustrator
Tove Jansson publishes the adventures of her creations, the Moomin.

1947   The Paris Peace Treaty of 1947 orders Finland to give up Karelia and part of Lapland
to the Soviet Union and to pay $300 million to the Soviets.

1952   Finland hosts the Olympic Games in Helsinki. Armi Kuusela of Finland wins the first-
ever Miss Universe beauty contest.

1955   The film of the Finnish novel *The Unknown Soldier* is released.

1969   Neutral Finland hosts the Strategic Arms Limitation Talks (SALT), aimed to reduce the
Cold War buildup of nuclear arms.

1991   The Soviet Union breaks apart, and Finland's economy suffers from the loss of its
major trade partner. The government takes steps to lower the suicide rate among
Finnish teens.

1995   Finland becomes a member of the European Union. Finland wins the World Ice Hockey
Championships.

2000   Finland swears in its first female president, Tarja Halonen.

2007   A student shoots eight people to death and then himself at Jokela high school.

2008   Former president of Finland Martti Ahtisaari wins the Nobel Peace Prize.
Apocalyptica becomes the first Finnish band to reach no. 1 on the U.S. *Billboard*
rock chart.

2009   Nokia, Finland's largest corporation, releases mini-laptops called booklets. A
shipyard at Turku completes the world's largest cruise ship.

2010   Finland's men's ice hockey team wins a bronze medal at the Winter
Olympics. Ash from a volcano erupting in Iceland temporarily closes
Finland's airports.

COUNTRY NAME Republic of Finland

AREA 130,128 square miles (337,030 sq. km)

MAIN LANDFORMS Åland Islands, Coastal Lowlands, Lake District, Salpausselkä Ridge, Turku Archipelago, Uplands

HIGHEST POINT Haltiatunturi, 4,344 feet (1,324 m) above sea level

MAJOR RIVERS Kemi, Muonio, Oulu, Saimaa Canal (human-made), Tornio

ANIMALS brown bears, elk, foxes, lemming, moose, muskrats, pine martens, reindeer, red squirrels, Saimaa ringed seal, wolves; cormorants, divers, eagles, grouse, hawks, owls, ptarmigan, storm petrels, swans, vultures, wild ducks; Baltic herring, codfish, eel, flounder, perch, pike, salmon, sea trout

CAPITAL CITY Helsinki

OTHER MAJOR CITIES Espoo, Oulu, Rovaniemi, Tampere, Turku

OFFICIAL LANGUAGES Finnish and Swedish

MONETARY UNITY euro (EUR); 100 cents = 1 euro

FINNISH CURRENCY

Finland adopted the euro in 1999. Euro banknotes, or paper money, come in seven different colors and denominations: 5, 10, 20, 50, 100, 200, and 500 euros. The eight coins are worth 1 and 2 euro, and then 1, 2, 5, 10, 20, and 50 cents. Each country that uses the euro provides its own national design for one side of the coin and uses a shared design on the other. Finland's national designs include the lion. Two flying swans grace the 1-euro coin, and cloudberries and their flowers appear on the 2-euro coin.

Finland's flag is a bright blue cross on a white field. The upright arm of the cross sits slightly off center, closer to the flag's hoist (left-hand) side. White represents the nation's snow, as well as peace and honesty. Blue represents Finland's lakes and sky. It also symbolizes justice and perseverance.

Finland's national anthem is not set by law, but tradition has firmly set "Our Country" in place. Musicians first performed the song in 1848, when Finland was still part of Sweden. It marked the beginning of Finnish national identity. The song's title is "Maamme" in Finnish and "Vårt land" in Swedish. Fredrik Pacius wrote the patriotic music. It has two sets of lyrics, one in Finnish and one in Swedish. The Swedish lyrics are from the heroic ballad *The Tales of Ensign Stål* by Johan Ludvig Runeberg. The Finnish lyrics are from Finnish poet Paavo Cajander's translation. Some Finns want to change the anthem to a section of Jean Sibelius's *Finlandia*, but "Our Country" remains the popular choice. The following is the English translation of the Finnish lyrics:

O our home country, Finland, the land where we were born,
sound high, you golden word!
There is no valley, no mountain,
no lake or shore more dear,
than this northern home,
the land of our fathers.

There shall be a time
when you will burst
into full blossom,
then our love shall be roused
by your glorious hope and joy,
at last, your song, o motherland,
will sound in higher tone!

 For a link to a site where you can listen to Finland's national anthem, "Our Country," visit www.vgsbooks.com.

Famous People

MARTTI AHTISAARI (b. 1937) Ahtisaari was born in Viipuri (Vyborg), which the Soviet Union took over when he was a child. He taught grade school before becoming a diplomat in 1965. As Finland's president from 1994 to 2000, he led Finland into the European Union. In 2008 Ahtisaari won the Nobel Peace Prize.

MARCUS GRÖNHOLM (b. 1968) Born in Kauniainen, Grönholm wanted to be a rally driver even though his father was killed in a motorsport accident. Grönholm won the World Rally Championship two times, in 2000 and 2002. In 2009 he called the 12-mile (20 km) race up the steep Pikes Peak Highway in Colorado—with 156 turns—his most challenging course yet.

TARJA HALONEN (b. 1943) Halonen was born in Helsinki. She studied literature and law at the University of Helsinki. She was Finland's foreign minister from 1995 until 2000, when she became president. Her friendly representation of her nation made her popular. As president, Halonen is part of the Council of Women World Leaders.

MAIJA ISOLA (1927–2001) Isola was born in Riihimäki and studied art at Helsinki Art School. A painter and designer, she created more than five hundred fabric patterns for the Finnish company Marimekko. Isola found inspiration for her work in Finland's nature and her world travels. Her bright, bold, and original patterns reflected the progressive mood of the 1960s.

TOVE JANSSON (1914–2001) Author and illustrator of the Moomin books and comic strip, Jansson was born in Helsinki. She published her first drawing when she was fourteen. Depressed by World War II, she created the gentle but strange Moomin, who look like hippos. Films, songs, and even a FinnAir airplane feature the characters.

AKI KAURISMÄKI (b. 1957) One of Finland's leading film directors, Kaurismäki was born in Helsinki. His films take a sympathetic and sometimes funny look at people on the edges of Finnish society. He first gained fame outside Finland with his film *Leningrad Cowboys Go America* (1989). It follows a fictional band. Kaurismäki film *The Man Without a Past* competed for the 2003 Academy Award for Best Foreign Language Film.

CARL GUSTAV EMIL MANNERHEIM (1867–1951) Born near Turku, when Finland was part of the Russian Empire, Mannerheim served in the Russian army for thirty years. He led the White troops to victory in Finland's 1918 Civil War. Between the world wars, he set up the Mannerheim League for Child Welfare and became chair of the Finnish Red Cross. After the Soviet attack of 1939, he took command of Finland's armed forces. His country gave him the special title Marshal of Finland on his seventy-fifth birthday.

KARITA MATTILA (b. 1960) Born in Somero, Mattila is one of the world's best opera singers. Music critics call her soprano voice rich, passionate, and electrifying. In 2010 she played the lead in a new production of the tragic opera *Tosca* at the Metropolitan Opera in New York City.

JORMA OLLILA (b. 1950) Born in Seinäjoki, Ollila is one of the most successful businesspeople in the world. As a student, he studied engineering. He became the CEO of the struggling Nokia Corporation in 1992. Ollila saw the possibilities of the new mobile technology, and he guided Nokia to world leadership in the cell phone and telecommunications business.

TANJA POUTIAINEN (b. 1980) A world-class alpine, or downhill, skier, Poutiainen was born in Rovaniemi. She competed in her first Alpine World Cup events in 1997. In 2006 she won a silver medal in the women's giant slalom at the Olympic Winter Games. Poutiainen lives and trains near the mountains of Switzerland.

JEAN SIBELIUS (1865–1957) Born in Hämeenlinna, Sibelius is Finland's most famous composer of classical music. He wrote a total of seven symphonies, as well as many songs and other pieces of music. Some Finns suggest using his piece *Finlandia* as the national anthem. Sibelius drew inspiration from other European musicians and especially from Finland's nature.

LINUS TORVALDS (b. 1969) Born in Helsinki, Torvalds studied computer science at the University of Helsinki. When he was twenty-one, he wrote the kernel, or central part, of a computer operating system. He made the system—called Linux—"open source." That is, he shared it for free on the Internet and invited anyone to help improve it. In 2006 *Time* magazine named him one of Europe's heroes. Linus's wife, Tove Torvalds, is a Finnish karate champion.

NILS-ASLAK VALKEAPÄÄ (1943–2001) A Sami musician, writer, and painter, Valkeapää was born in Enontekiö, Lapland. He came from a family of traditional reindeer herders and became a schoolteacher. Valkeapää was a key figure in the revival of Sami culture. In the 1960s, his performances and recordings of yoik, the traditional Sami song style, were key to saving the dying musical form. Valkeapää acted in and wrote the music for the 1987 film *Ofelaš* (*Pathfinder*). The Norwegian film retold an old Sami legend.

ATENEUM ART MUSEUM One of about forty museums in Helsinki, this collection displays art from Finland's Golden Age (the decades around 1900). Don't miss Askeli Gallen-Kallela's three-panel painting from the *Kalevala*, showing the hero's chase of the maiden Aino. Many Finns' choose this triptych as their favorite Finnish work of art.

KEMI SNOWCASTLE AND ARTIC ICEBREAKER In the harbor town of Kemi is one of Finland's biggest wintertime attractions: the world's largest snow castle. Built anew every year, it has a chapel, sculptures, and a restaurant, all made of ice. Guests can stay overnight (in Artic sleeping bags) at the ice hotel. In Kemi you can also take a four-hour trip on the only icebreaking ship that accepts passengers.

LINNANMÄKI AMUSEMENT PARK This Helsinki park is the number one destination for children in Finland. The wooden roller coaster from the 1950s is its most popular ride. Though it is safe, its creaky sounds are very scary. Environmentally friendly hydropower fuels all the rides.

LUSTO, THE FINNISH FOREST MUSEUM This unique museum in the Saimaa lake district shows the significance of forests in Finnish life through exhibitions and events. Demonstrations include sculpting wood with chain saws and making pine tar.

NUUKSIO NATIONAL PARK This protected wilderness forest and lake area in Espoo is ideal for short hiking and camping trips. It is the national park nearest Helsinki. Visitors can escape the city for a day to pick wild berries and mushrooms. In winter the nature trails become cross-country ski paths. Elk, woodpeckers, and flying squirrels are among the many animals that live in the park.

SIIDA: SAMI MUSEUM AND NORTHERN LAPLAND NATURE CENTER Siida is located in the small village of Inari, known for its genuine Sami arts. This museum brings Sami culture to life with events and changing displays. Excellent exhibits feature the nature of the Arctic, such as the northern lights and Arctic foxes. The open-air part of the museum displays typical Sami dwellings and hunting methods, including bear and wolf traps.

TURKU ARCHIPELAGO One of the best ways to explore this scenic group of twenty thousand islands, south of Turku, is to bike around the 124-mile (200 km) Archipelago Ring Road. You can visit museums, go fishing (or just eat fresh fish), visit a potter's workshop, or stop at the Moomin-themed amusement park Moominworld in the port city of Naantali.

détente: from a French word meaning "to relax," a policy to ease or lessen the tensions between hostile superpowers (the United States and the Soviet Union) during the Cold War

European Union (EU): a group of nations in Europe that agreed in 1993 to unite their markets so that people, trade goods, services, and money could move freely across borders. The union's goal is to strengthen the European economy and to reduce tensions between nations. By 2010 twenty-seven nations had become EU members. Sixteen of these, including Finland, share a common currency called the euro.

gross domestic product (GDP): the value of the goods and services a country produces over a period of time, usually one year

literacy: the ability to read and write a basic sentence

Nordic: refers to the region and people of Northern Europe and the North Atlantic. The Nordic nations are the Scandinavian countries (Denmark, Norway, and Sweden), Finland, and the island nation of Iceland. Nordic nations share certain social and political values, including guaranteeing basic human rights for all.

northern lights: also called the aurora borealis, these colorful lights are visible in the winter nighttime sky in Finland and other northern places. Finns call the lights fox fire. They are the result of electrified particles colliding in the atmosphere, near Earth's magnetic poles.

parliament: a legislature, or group of lawmakers. The name comes from the French word *parler*, which means "to speak." Each member of parliament is called a minister. The prime minister is usually the leader of the main party, who serves as the country's head of government.

postglacial rebound: the gradual rise of land from the sea, after the heavy ice pressing the land down melted at the end of the last ice age

Sami: the indigenous, or native, people of Lapland, who live in the far north of Finland, Norway, Sweden, and Russia. In the past, Sami were called Lapps, but the Sami consider this word a little insulting.

sauna: of ancient Finnish origins, a sauna is a room or small building that is heated to 140 to 210°F (60 to 99°C). After about fifteen minutes in the heat, sauna users cool off in a lake or shower. Many Finns take a sauna at least once a week, for health and relaxation.

sisu: a Finnish word that means something like "guts" in the face of hardship. Many Finns consider this brave, never-give-up attitude to be a national trait.

British Broadcasting Corporation. BBC News. 2009.
http://news.bbc.co.uk/ (November 2009).
The BBC covers news from Finland and around the world. Its site contains regularly updated political and cultural news. The BBC's country profile of Finland is at http://news.bbc.co.uk/2/hi/europe/country_profiles/1023629 .stm.

Central Intelligence Agency. "The World Factbook–Finland." *The World Factbook*. **2009.**
https://www.cia.gov/library/publications/the-world-factbook/geos/fi.html (October 2009).
The United States CIA provides this general profile of Finland. The profile includes brief summaries of the nation's geography, people, government, economy, communications, transportation, and military.

The Europa World Year Book, 2009. **London: Routledge, 2009.**
This annual publication provides accurate, current information on Finland and other countries of the world. It covers the country's recent history, economic affairs, government, education, statistics on health and welfare, and more.

Federal Research Division, Library of Congress. *A Country Study: Finland*. **Washington, DC: Federal Research Division, Library of Congress, 1988.**
This study of Finland covers its history in depth, up to 1988. The book also covers Finland's society, culture, economy, government, and politics. The complete text is available online at http://lcweb2.loc.gov/frd/cs/fitoc.html.

Finland: A Cultural Encyclopedia. **Olli Alho, ed. Helsinki: Finnish Literary Society, 1999.**
Photos and charts illustrate this book's in-depth articles on Finland's vital artistic life. Coverage includes the way of life, customs, the food, and leisure activities, as well as the standard arts of literature and design.

Kirby, David. *A Concise History of Finland*. **Cambridge: Cambridge University Press, 2006.**
Kirby is a history professor whose book shows in-depth how Finland developed its own unique identity after years of foreign rule.

Lavery, Jason. *The History of Finland*. **Westport, CT: Greenwood, 2006.**
An analytical look at Finland's history, this book covers the country's prehistoric origins all the way to the Finnish band Lordi's victory at the Eurovision song contest in 2006.

Maude, George. *Historical Dictionary of Finland*. **Lanham, MD: Scarecrow Press, 2007.**
This reference work reveals Finnish history through hundred of dictionary entries covering important people, places, and events, and aspects of the economy, the society, and the culture.

Ministry of Justice, Finland. *The Constitution of Finland.* **June 11, 1999. February 22, 2007.**
http://www.om.fi/21910.htm (November 1, 2009).
The complete text of Finland's constitution, translated into English, is provided here. The document is the foundation of the country's laws and outlines its governmental system. This page also links to more information about the Finnish government.

Population Reference Bureau. "Data Finder: Finland." Population Reference Bureau (PRB).
http://www.prb.org/Datafinder 2009. (October 2009).
A wealth of population, demographic, and health statistics for Finland and almost all countries in the world can be found on this site. PRB also provides in-depth articles about conditions around the world.

Symington, Andy. *Finland.* **Footscray, Victoria, Australia: Lonely Planet, 2006.**
Besides travel tips, this guidebook includes entertaining and informative sections on Finland's history and culture. Maps, sidebars, and photos round out the text.

Thompson, Wayne C. *Western Europe, 2009.* **Harpers Ferry, WV: Stryker-Post, 2009.**
The long article on Finland in this book in the annual World Today series covers the country's history, economy, and culture.

Turner, Barry, ed. *The Statesman's Yearbook: The Politics, Cultures and Economies of the World, 2010.* **New York: Macmillan, 2009.**
This annual publication provides concise information on Finland's history, climate, government, economy, and culture, including relevant statistics.

U.S. Department of State. "Background Notes: Finland." U.S. Department of State. 2009.
http://www.state.gov/r/pa/ei/bgn/3238.htm (October 2009).
This website provides a general profile of Finland, from the U.S. Department of State. The profile includes brief summaries of the nation's geography, people, government and politics, and economy.

Books from Finland: A Literary Journal of Writing from and about Finland.
http://www.booksfromfinland.fi
On this online English-language magazine, you can read complete poems, parts of books, and interviews with authors from Finland. Information about Finnish books and authors, both classic and modern, is also available.

Clark, Geri. *Finland*. New York: Children's Press, 2009.
Part of the Enchantment of the World series, this book for younger readers describes the geography, the history, the culture, the industry, and the people of Finland.

Food from Finland
http://www.foodfromfinland.com
Food from Finland is dedicated to Finnish food and food culture. The website offers photographs and many wonderful recipes. The measurements, however, are in metric units. You can find an international conversion calculator for cooks here: http://www.vegalicious.org/international-conversion-calculator.

Jansson, Tove. *Finn Family Moomintroll*. New York: Farrar, Straus and Giroux, 1990.
This collection of stories is a good place to enter into Jansson's classic tales of the Moomin—strange, endearing creatures that look like hippos. They are well loved in Finland by children and adults.

Kaj Stenvall
http://www.kajstenvall.com/
You can see Kaj Stenvall's popular cartoon-duck paintings at his site.

Kristiina Uusitalo
http://www.kristiinauusitalo.fi/
Uusitalo employs some Asian brush-painting techniques in her large paintings of the Finnish landscape, which you can see on her site.

Leney, Terttu. *Finland: A Quick Guide to Customs and Etiquette*. Portland, OR: Graphic Arts Publishing, 2005.
A guide to Finnish values and attitudes, this book is fun and informative. The author describes sisu—that Finnish gutsy pride—as well as details of daily life, such as how much coffee the average Finn drinks.

Makinen, Kirsti. *The Kalevala: Tales of Magic and Adventure*. Vancouver, BC: Simply Read Books, 2009.
The Kalevala is one of the most important works of Finnish literature. Elias Lonnröt originally gathered its ancient tales in the nineteenth century. This English translation and its magical illustrations are aimed at young adults. Beginning with the world's creation, the book follows the stories of the hero, Väinämöinen, and his young rival on their quests for love, revenge, and truth. You can read an old English translation of the original *Kalevala* online: http://www.sacred-texts.com/neu/kveng.

Ojakangas, Beatrice A. *The Finnish Cookbook*. New York: Crown, 1989.

Personal tales and interesting tidbits go along with recipes for dishes every Finn would know, including Finnish cinnamon rolls. Unlike most online recipe sources, this book provides measurements in U.S. units (teaspoons, cups, etc.), not the metric weights Finns and other Europeans use.

Robinson, Deborah. *The Sami of Northern Europe*. Minneapolis: Lerner Publications Company, 2002.

This book describes both the traditional and modern lifeways of the Sami, the indigenous people of northern Finland and other parts of northern Europe.

Sami Culture
http://www.utexas.edu/courses/sami/ .

The University of Texas offers classes and provides an extensive website about the Sami, the indigenous people of Lapland. This site offers a wealth of articles, photos, art, audio clips, and film links.

The Sami Yoik
http://www.utexas.edu/courses/sami/diehtu/giella/music/yoiksunna.htm

You can listen to several audios of yoik singing here. The text provides a good overview of the songs' role in Sami religion and worldview. Click on a link to watch *Yoik*, a half-hour film of Sami yoikers performing in 2005.

Tam Chung Lee. *Finland*. New York: Marshall Cavendish, 1996.

Part of the Cultures of the World series, this book for younger readers offers an introduction to the geography, the history, the government, the economy, the people, and the culture of Finland.

thisisFINLAND
http://finland.fi/public/

Produced by the Ministry for Foreign Affairs of Finland and published by the Finland Promotion Board, thisisFINLAND is a window on Finland for everyone interested in the country, its culture, and its people. It covers anything related to Finland and Finnish society.

vgsbooks.com
http://www.vgsbooks.com

Visit vgsbooks.com, the home page of the Visual Geography Series®, which is updated regularly. You can get linked to all sorts of useful online information, including geographical, historical demographic, cultural, and economic websites. The vgsbooks.com site is a great resource for late-breaking news and statistics.

Visit Finland
http://www.visitfinland.com/en_US/web/guest/finland-guide/home

This is the portal of the Finnish Tourism Board. Find out what to see and do in Finland, whether you want to take a hot-air balloon trip over the Arctic or attend a tango festival.

Captions for photos appearing on cover and chapter openers:

Cover: The SnowCastle at Kemi, Finland, on the Gulf of Bothnia is built every January and open to tourists until mid-April. The castle has a hotel, a restaurant, and a chapel open daily.

pp. 4–5 The Market Square in Helsinki—Finland's capital—is a popular destination for Finns and tourists alike.

pp. 8–9 The Haukkalampi pond is one of thirty-eight lakes and ponds in Nuuksio National Park.

pp. 20–21 Built on a group of rocky islands off the coast of Helsinki, the Suomenlinna Fortress played an important role in Finland's military history. As a UNESCO World Heritage Site, it is one of Finland's most popular tourist attractions.

pp. 38–39 Families picnic at Kaivopuisto Park in Helsinki to celebrate Vappu, a Finnish national holiday on May 1. Finns welcome the coming of spring by gathering with family and friends over food and drink.

pp. 46–47 The internationally famous rock band Apocalyptica performs on cellos in Helsinki.

pp. 58–59 A wooden boardwalk leads to the entrance of the ultramodern Nokia headquarters in Espoo, Finland.